# UNCOLLECTED POEMS

BY

## SAMUEL ROWLANDS

# Uncollected Poems

(1604?-1617)

*Humors Ordinarie (1604?)*
*A Theater of Delightfull Recreation (1605)*
*Humors Antique Faces (1605)*
*The Bride (1617)*

By

## Samuel Rowlands

Facsimile Reproductions

With an Introduction

By

## Frederick O. Waage, Jr.

*Four Volumes in one*

Gainesville, Florida

Scholars' Facsimiles & Reprints

1970

SCHOLARS' FACSIMILES & REPRINTS

1605 N.W. 14TH AVENUE

GAINESVILLE, FLORIDA 32601 U.S.A.

HARRY R. WARFEL, GENERAL EDITOR

Grateful acknowledgment is made for permission received from the following libraries to reprint the following books in their collections:

Folger Shakespeare Library and the "Bishop Percy Library" in the Department of Special Collections of the Library of the Queen's University of Belfast, Ireland: *A Theater of Delightfull Recreation.*

The Henry E. Huntington Library and Art Gallery: *Humors Ordinarie* and *Humors Antique Faces.*

The Houghton Library of Harvard University: *The Bride.*

L.C. CATALOG CARD NUMBER: 74-119867

ISBN 8201-1074-4

MANUFACTURED IN THE U.S.A.

# CONTENTS

# INTRODUCTION

The four books of poetry here reprinted are the only ones convincingly attributed to Samuel Rowlands which do not appear in the sole collected edition of his work, that issued by the Hunterian Club in three volumes in 1880, which was a limited edition. Only one of them has been printed in full elsewhere, namely *The Bride*, in 1905, with an introduction by Alfred C. Potter. That edition was also limited. I feel these four works should be available, in order that Rowlands's career may be more fully understood, as well as those of the many neglected "popular" writers of his time.

Samuel Rowlands was one of a group of Renaissance writers presently styled "popular" or "professional," whose works are often neglected or not taken seriously because of the circumstances of their composition, the audience for which they were intended, or the social position and acquaintances of their authors. The intrinsic interest and value of satires, narrative poems, tracts by a Rowlands, a Brathwaite, or a John Taylor are too often confused with unclearly defined normative criteria external to the works themselves.

In the case of Rowlands, at least, little is known even of the externals of his career. The following facts and speculations presented by Edmund Gosse in his 1880 Introduction to the Hunterian Club edition of Rowlands can scarcely be expanded upon today: Rowlands may have been born around 1570, may have died around 1630, seems to have lived all his life in London and never to have attended a university, and (from allusions in his works) seems to have had a particular interest in and dislike for the theater. Little higher value has been put upon his work than that accorded by Sir Edmund: "he is a kind of small, non-political Defoe, a pamphleteer in verse whose talents were never put into exercise except when their possessor was pressed for means, and a poet of considerable talent without one spark or glimmer of genius." The only significant variation on this judgment is that of Sarah Dickson, "The 'Humours' of Samuel Rowlands," *PBSA*, XLIV (1950), 101-117, who considers him "the most undeservedly neglected of Jacobean writers." This facsimile edition of four of his works hitherto unreprinted is intended to reduce this neglect.

A review of Rowlands's total *oeuvre* shows a meaningful evolution in his ideas and literary technique— an evolution rarely attributed to "professional" writers. He began his career, as did many of his contemporaries, with a "safe" devotional work. This was the sententious Biblical elaboration and paraphrase, *The Betraying of Christ* (1598), one of many blasts for divine, against the currently best-selling erotic, verse— but which is as well both a holy "Mirror," featuring the treachery of Judas confessed by the sinner himself in the manner of *St. Peter's Complaint*, and a political comment on the current rebellion in Ireland. For his next publication Rowlands chose a complementary genre of moral exhortation in great favor in the 1590's, satire, and composed the verses of the famous *The Letting of Humours Blood in the Head-Vaine* (1600), ordered burned by the Stationers' Company (see below); in 1602 he used the "slice of life" social realism of Robert Greene (who is amusingly lauded in its preface) for *'Tis Merry When Gossips Meet,* a trialogue in the jig tradition between a Widow, a Wife, and a Maid, where he first shows his sympathy and respect for the woman's role in the troublesome institution of marriage. The same year saw *Greene's Ghost Haunting Cony-Catchers,* a slavish imitation of the Master, much plagiarized from him and from *other* imitators. In 1603 *Ave Caesar: God Save the King* joined the many other encomiums on the new sovereign but, unlike most, expressed only a wary hope, rather than an enthusiastic certainty, that he heralded a new Golden Age.

After James's accession Rowlands's writing distinctly divides into two main strains. The first is that of satire. *Looke to It, or Ile Stabbe Ye* (1604), with its theme of Death the great annihilator of Time and all Time's creatures, initiates a series of less somber verse sketches, tales, and characters which includes *Diogines Lanthorne* (1607), *Humors Looking Glasse* (1608), *Doctor Merrie-Man* (1609), *A Whole Crew of Kind Gossips* (1609), *The Knave of Clubbes* (1609), *The Knave of Harts* (1612), *More Knaves Yet?* (1613), *A Fooles Bolt is Soone Shott* (1614), *The Night-Raven* (1620), and *A Paire of Spy-Knaves* (1620?).

Secondly, setting aside his neo-romance of *Guy of Warwick* (1609), his all-time best-seller (with at least nine editions before 1700), and the 1605 highwayman pamphlets *The Life and Death of Gamaliel Ratsey* and *Ratseis Ghost,* ascribed to Rowlands by J. L. Lievsay on what seem to me vague and insufficient grounds, there remains an interesting series of serious writings descending from *The Betraying of Christ,* most of which use the "Mirror" convention in various ways to comment on the human condition. The first is the plague-inspired verse morality *A Terrible Battell betweene the Two Consumers of the Whole World: Time and Death* (before 1605). The paradoxical interdependence and enmity of these two great Ultimate Figures seemingly illustrates man's uncertainty about whether meaning should be found in this world or in the next; *Hell's Broke Loose* (1605), inspired by the Gunpowder Plot, is a Mirror-type verse history of the revolutionary Anabaptist John Leyden, who embodies the chaotic consequences of choosing this world and illusory freedom from God. *A Theater of Delightfull Recreation* (1605; see below) is for Rowlands the *magnum opus* which resolves the "terrible battell" in favor of order and God; its publication was followed by nearly a decade of intellectual quiescence during which Rowlands wrote only ephemeral satires. But by 1613 ominous events including the murder of Sir Thomas Overbury, covered up by official hypocrisy, had inspired Rowlands to compose an eloquent broadside, "Sir Thomas Overbury, or, the Poysoned Knight's Complaint," wherein the as yet unpunished crime casts doubt on divine justice. The broadside's implicit skepticism is deepened in the satiric *The Melancholy Knight* (1615) where through his Browningesque soliloquy the knight comes to represent the illusory nature of any order by which men give meaning to their lives and justify their actions. The Bride (1617; discussed below) precedes Rowlands's two final serious writings, *A Sacred Memorie of the Miracles wrought by our Lord and Saviour Jesus Christ* (1618), and *Heavens Glory, seeke it. Earths Vanitie, flye it. Hells horror, feare it* (1628), which resolve the worldly doubts of the melancholy knight into a morally coherent world, given spiritual meaning through Christ's redemptive intervention.  Rowlands's career thus ends where it began, on a note of Puritan inspiration, although its interest derives from the dark passages of questioning on the road to this happy goal.

First among the works here reprinted, *Humors Ordinarie* (1604?) is really the second—disguised and altered—edition of Samuel Rowlands's notorious book of satires and epigrams, *The Letting of Humours Blood in the Head Vaine.*  The Huntington Library copy of that edition here reprinted is undated, but such details as the changing of "Queen's highway" to "King's highway" in Epigram Three suggest a date after James's accession in 1603 and before the next— dated—edition of 1607 (two more editions followed, in 1611 and 1613, with the original title restored). The use of the original rather than the altered title for the work in the list of books repudiated by Row- lands in *A Theater of Delightfull Recreation* (1605) could mean that Rowlands still thought, and was proud, of his new book under its old name, or else that it had not been reissued yet as *Humors Ordinarie.*

Rowlands's original *Letting of Humours Blood* was ordered burned by the Bishop of London (June 1, 1599) along with fourteen booksellers' stocks of other current satires, *before* it was successfully licensed (October 16, 1600) and all copies of it subsequently ordered destroyed by the Court of the Stationers' Company (October 24, 1600).  Long after twenty- eight booksellers were fined two shillings sixpence each on March 4, 1600-01 for buying it, it was reissued as *Humors Ordinarie* and the introductory verses spoken by Satir, the Vintner, were added.  Strangely, Rowlands's name was still prominent on the second page.  Perhaps the official censorship of these rela- tively innocuous verses, and the booksellers' per- sistence in evading it, were due to the nation's insecur-

ity at the time of the Earl of Essex's rebellion and
execution, when Rowlands's book was on sale. Any
general criticism of England was considered part of
some "popishe" plot (*Humours Blood* was to be
burned "with other popishe bookes and thinges" ac-
cording to the Stationers' order), yet popular sym-
pathy for martyred Essex made books of public criti-
cism best-sellers to be kept in the stalls.

From a literary point of view, *Humors Ordinarie*
differs from *The Letting of Humours Blood* only in its
structural metaphor of the book as an unholy temple
to drunkenness, established by Satir's preface. A
probable direct source for this framing device is, as
E. M. Waith suggests in *RES*, XVIII (1942), 218,
Thomas Dekker's Boccacian *The Meeting of Gallants
at an Ordinarie* (1604). The form allows satiric com-
ments to be "overheard" in the place, not experienced
as direct authorial attacks in the earlier Marstonian
manner, and since they are based on an assumed
moral code from which the present has fallen away
rather than on the emotional outrage of the "bitter"
satirist, the book signals a general trend towards
morality-oriented satire and away from "realism" and
cynicism. It presents virtue and vice through por-
traits of humourous "characters," but recognizes that
men are "humourous" because of their new and dis-
turbing desire to be recognized for their individual,
not their common, characteristics. Thus Rowlands's
ordinary is the nascent modern world where men get
drunk on ambition and self-esteem, qualities which
his contemporary William Perkins copes with, in a
contrary way, by putting them in a Puritan temple.

Rowlands's *A Theater of Delightfull Recreation*
(1605) was written to echo in title and subject some
of the most respected books of his time, and it should
be considered his *magnum opus*. Until recently, the

sole surviving copy was thought to be the Folger Shakespeare Library copy (the work is absent from the *Short Title Catalog*), but a second copy, from Bishop Percy's collection, sold at Sotheby's on June 23, 1969, is now at Queen's University, Belfast, Northern Ireland. Facsimiles below of pages fifty-six through sixty-one are from this latter copy, as these pages are missing from the Folger copy. Otherwise the only significant difference between the two seems to be a sheet inserted following the title-page in the Queen's University copy, which bears a signed dedication by Samuel Rowlands to "The Right Worshipfull Tobie Woode Esquire."

The work, meant for the most part to apply the monitory function of the *Mirror for Magistrates* to *divine* history, was entered in the *Stationers' Register* as *A Theater of Divine Recreation* on October 8, 1605, and is divided roughly into three sections: introductory material consisting of an epistle to the reader, an invocation of the Muses, and verses to the author; a series of versified incidents from the Old Testament; and, finally, miscellaneous divine poems in a *contemptus mundi* vein.

The first section of the *Theater* is a contribution to the Puritan-inspired literature of personal confession: the opening address to the reader, repudiating the author's previous unholy writings, draws its appeal from similar retractions made by Robert Greene (the archetypal penitent), Stephen Gosson, and Joseph Hall. As a demonstration of *redemptio temporis*, it echoes Anthony Munday's penitent *A Second and Third Blast of Retraite from Plaies and Theaters*. The commendatory verses by Rowlands's friends show an understanding of his redemptive purpose and the controlling metaphoric contrast between a divine and a profane stage play (an extension of the ancient

tavern-church dichotomy in *Humors Ordinarie*). Two
of the commenders are themselves known to litera-
ture: Rowlands contributed verses to Thomas An-
drewe's *The Unmasking of a Feminine Machiavel*
(1604), and "I.G." is probably the author of *An Apolo-
gie for Womenkinde* (1605), dealing with one of
Rowlands's favorite themes.

The second part of Rowlands's *Theater* draws on
and vulgarizes several current literary forms and con-
ventions.  One is that of the emblem-book, in the
manner of Jan Van der Noot's *Theater for Worldlings*:
the pictures accompanying the texts make the book a
theater, where the audience can *see* as well as *hear*.
In Rowlands's *Theater* the "pictures" are the Biblical
events described, standing out timelessly in the flux of
human history, but Rowlands's Pharoah or his Absalom
are presented more vividly and dramatically than they
are in Anthony Munday's similar (and earlier) at-
tempt to extend the *Mirror for Magistrates* into Old
Testament times, his *The Mirrour of Mutabilitie*
(1579).  If Rowlands owes his basic idea of a Bibli-
cal Mirror to Munday, he may have been inspired to
frame its incidents between the two ultimate events
of human history, Adam's fall and Christ's death, by
Francis Sabie's *Adams Complaint* (1596), which fol-
lows a similar pattern.  Thomas Beard's *Theater of
God's Judgements* (1597), with its Puritan emphasis
on the immediate relevance of God's past judgments
to the present corrupt world, lies behind Rowlands's
decision to place his Mirror in the context of his own
personal repentance of past errors; repentance is the
means, made possible by Christ's sacrifice, by which
he can evade God's judgment.  Most important, per-
haps, as an influence on Rowlands's *Theater* was *Du
Bartas his Divine Weekes and Works*, first published
as a unit in Sylvester's translation just a few months

before the appearance of the *Theater*.  Other writers
like Nicholas Breton joined Rowlands in paying trib-
ute to Du Bartas's muse of divine poetry, Urania, who
patronized his "new" Protestant verse that was to re-
place the pagan epic.

Fittingly, in his final section of the *Theater*, Row-
lands balances the recital of man's punishments under
the old law with that of his rewards under the new.
Starting with Christ's Passion, he goes on to contrast
Solomon's wordly harlot to his worshipful housewife,
who in marriage restores the mutuality of unfallen
Adam and Eve; similarly he contrasts the eternal New
Jerusalem to the mutable world.  He concludes by
describing the Last Judgement in the form of a per-
sonal prayer, thereby reconciling his frail individuality
with the world's order, and mortality with eternity.

The anonymous satiric pamphlet *Humors Antique
Faces* (1605) was first attributed to Rowlands by E.
M. Waith in 1942, and the attribution was more firmly
established by Sarah Dickson in 1950.  Waith be-
lieved it to be a differently-titled first edition of Row-
lands's 1608 pamphlet, *Humors Looking Glasse*, and
found nine identical poems in the two, many precise
verbal parallels, and Rowlands's style and attitude—
all of which he felt outweighed the signature "E. M."
at the end of the last poem.  We may add that in the
1605 *Theater* Rowlands repudiated *Humors Looking
Glasse* ("I'll show no more to each fantastique asse/
His pourtraicture in Humour's Looking Glasse"), so
there must have been an edition of it earlier than the
first one preserved—explaining, perhaps, as Waith
suggests, why *Humors Looking Glasse* was not en-
tered in the *Stationers' Register* in 1608.  Is *Humors
Antique Faces* the same as this earlier edition, but re-
ferred to by Rowlands under its later name, or was it
issued separately, with author and title disguised, to

conceal a violation of his pledge no longer to be a humorist?

Rowlands's pamphlet, in title and content, evokes the Jonsonian stage-comedy, a mirror in which the distorted features are the audience's own, reflected back for their edification. Rowlands's Oberon, like Greene's in the "frame" of *James IV*, takes the responsibility for his satire off the writer by conventionally charging him (as Mirror characters do) with bearing higher truths to man. *Humors Antique Faces* is an antimasque, with man in the darkness deformed by the self-love satirized, and restored by the light of day —a pagan version, if you will, of the pattern of fall and redemption in the *Theater*. Oberon and his connotations are absent from *Humors Looking Glasse*, and that book's last nine epigrams are the only ones carried over from *Humors Antique Faces*. The new ones are more vivid and biting, showing perhaps Rowlands's freedom from the seriousness of self-concern that characterizes his *Theater* period.

Rowlands's *The Bride* (1617), whose 1905 editor, Alfred C. Potter, accorded it little value, continues the discussion of womanhood in *'Tis Merry When Gossips Meet, A Whole Crew of Kind Gossips*, and elsewhere, and is an interesting reflection of a controversy at the heart of the religious and social discord of the seventeenth century: what is the nature of "woman," what is her proper role in society, and as a wife in the most sacred social institution, the family? What sets Rowlands's dialogue apart from other contemporary discussions is that his women, supposedly innocent, ignorant virgins, are overheard discussing with self-determining rationality which role is best for them. Their earthiness rebukes the artificiality of the Spenserian epithalamic tradition, and the tortured metaphysics of Thomas Overbury's *A Wife* (1613). The conflict over female rationality and power was most visible in the drama. There the consequences of a hypothetical female freedom, in which the laws of Heinrich Bullinger's *Christian State of Matrimony* and Henry Smith's *Preparative to Marriage* did not apply, were explored in such plays as Dekker's *Honest Whore*, Marston's *Dutch Courtesan*, and Middleton's *Women Beware Women*. Many bourgeois wives caught the dangerous aristocratic infection of self-assertion, both on stage and off. Widespread mysogyny resulted from the fear that this disease might undermine the Biblical authority (in Paul and *Genesis*) on which social order was based. This mysogyny found its Bible in Joseph Swetnam's famous tirade, *An Arraignment of Lewd, Idle, Froward and Unconstant Women* (1615), which inspired, in 1617, three indignant female responses: Rachel Speght's *A Mouzell for Melastomus*, Esther Sowernam's *Ester Hath Hang'd Haman*, "Constantia Munda"'s *The Worming of a Madde Dogge*—and one more subtle male one, Rowlands's *The Bride*.

Rowlands's girls are as combative and opinionated as these three authoresses. His heroine, the bride, uses "the rules of reasons arte" to persuade the others that marriage is higher socially and more holy than virginity, which is no less than an active violation of God's command to man to increase. In this effort, she ironically uses arguments usually attributed to figures representing Lust, but she always associates "increase" with marriage, as though the possibility of extra-marital sex did not exist. In fact, both she and the main exponent of virginity, Mistris Susan, use freedom as the most attractive aspect of the states they favor. Although the pamphlet concludes with the bride's recitation of eight conventional wifely duties, to concentrate on them as its ultimate message, as Louis B.

Wright does in *Middle Class Culture in Elizabethan England,* is to neglect the real originality of the pamphlet. This originality lies in the idea of freedom as the important quality in whatever state is finally chosen as best, and in the technique of argument from the concrete and ambiguous grounds of psychological reality, not from the metaphysical absolutes and Biblical doctrines which are the only ammunition even of Rachel Speght, Esther Sowernam, and "Constantia Munda." Even the parodic tale of Merlin's mother, and the nearly Freudian dream-vision, used as the clinching arguments against Mistris Susan, embody a "reason" arising directly from experience and enshrined in parable through repeated confirmation in actual life-situations—a reason that escapes the traditional dualism, expressed in *Comus,* of corrupt reasoning in fallen man versus immediate vision of universal truth.

Rowlands's bride concludes: "The joyes of marriage I want art to tell, /and therefore no more talke, but try and prove." Her empirical way of viewing reality is what Bacon admired in Rowlands's class, free of the tyranny of idols over the understanding. Within the narrow limits of his intelligence and experience, Samuel Rowlands does discuss the broad concern of his age over the choice between God-centered and Man-centered universe, between divine and natural law. In this sense he transcends the "popular."

FREDERICK O. WAAGE, JR.

*Northwestern University*
*October 1, 1969*

# HVMORS

## ORDINARIE.

## VVhere a man may be

*verie merrie, and excee-
ding vvell vsed for his
Sixe-Pence*

AT LONDON,
*Printed for* William Firebrand, *and are to*
be fold at his fhop in Popeshead Pallace, right
ouer againft the Tauerne doore.

# TO THE GENTLE-
## men Readers.

HVmours, is late crown'd king of Caueeleres,
Fantastique-follies, grac'd commun fauour:
Ciuilitie, hath serued out his yeares,
And scorneth now to waite on good-behauieur.
Gallants, like Richard the Vsurper swagger.
That had his hand continuall on his dagger.

Fashions is still consort with new found shapes,
And feedeth daylie vpon strange disguise:
We shew our selues imitating Apes
Of all the toyes that Strangers heades deuise;
For ther's no habit of hell-hatched sinne,
That we delight not to be cloathed in.

Some sweare, as though they Stares from heauen could pull
And all their speech is pointed with the stabbe,
When all men know it is some coward gull,
That is but Champion to a Shordich drabbe.
Whose feather is his heades lightnes-proclaitter,
Although he seeme some mightie monster-tamer.

A 2

Epicu-

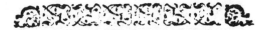

## To the Readers.

Epicuri∫me , *cares not how he liues,*
*But ∫till pur∫ueth brutish Appetite:*
Di∫daine ,*regardes not what abu∫e he giues ,*
Carele∫∫e of wrongs, *and ui regarding right,*
Selfe loue ,*( they ∫ay )to ∫elfe-conceit is wed,*
*By which ba∫e match are vgly vices bred.*

Pride ,*reuells like the roy∫ting Prodigall,*
*Stretching his credit that his pur∫e ∫trings cracke,*
*Vntill in ∫ome di∫tre∫∫full gaile he fall,*
*Which wore of late a Lord∫hip on his backe:*
*where he till death mu∫t lie in pawne for debt:*
"*Grie∫es night is neare ,when plea∫ures ∫un is ∫et.*

Vaunting, *hath got a mighty thundring voyce,*
*Looking that all men ∫hould applaude his ∫ound,*
*His deedes are ∫ingular , his words be choyce;*
*On earth his equall is not to be found.*
*Thus* Vertu's *hid with* Follies *iugling mi∫t,*
*And hees no man that is no humori∫t.*

Samuell Rovvlands.

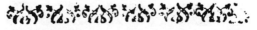

## TO POETS.

GOod honeſt Poets let me craue a boone,
    That you would write, I do not care how ſoon
Againſt the baſtard humors howrely bred,
In euery mad braind wit-worne, giddy head:
At ſuch groſſe follies doe not ſit and winke,
Belabour theſe ſame Gulls with pen and inke:
You ſee ſome ſtriue for faire hand-writing fame,
As *Peter Bales*, his ſigne can proue the ſame,
Gracing his credit with a golden Pen :
I would haue Poets proue more taller men:
In perfeẛt letters reſted his contention,
But yours conſiſts in Wits choiſe rare inuention.
Wil you ſtand ſpending your inuentions treaſure,
To teach Stage Parrets ſpeak for penny pleaſure?
While you your ſelues like muſick-ſoŭding Lutes
Fretted and ſtrung, gaine them their ſilken ſutes.
Leaue *Cupids* cut, womens face-flattring praiſe,
Loues ſubiẛt growes too threed-bare now adais.
Change *Venus* Swans, to write of *Vulcans* Geeſe,
And you ſhall merit golden Pennes a peece.

*Mirth pleaſeth ſome, to others t'is offence,*
    *Some wiſh t'haue follies told; ſome diſlike that:*
*Some commend plaine conceits, ſome profound ſenſe :*
*And moſt would haue, themſelues they know not what.*
*Then be that would pleaſe all, and himſelfe too,*
*Takes more in hand then he is like to doe.*

Euen

# SATIR.

EVen like the chalking Vintners at the barre,
That bids all welcome, what so e're they are:
So they passe quiet, in, and out a doore,
And make no swaggering to discharge their scoare
I Satir, stand at entrance of this booke,
And each kind guest may for my welcome looke:
All pleasant humours I inuite come here,
And with these Epigrams make the good cheere:
Let Melancholie walke most dogged by,
All sprightly Poets doe the same desie,
To feast with wit he neuer had good tast,
I scorne to haue him at our Table plast.
Let him goe plead for leases, buy and sell,
And day by day his bags of money tell,
And grudge to giue himselfe a pint of Wine,
Out arrant Asse, he is no guest of mine.
But all mirths friends, I doe embrace most kind,
Better I wish, pray take such as you find.

# EPIGRAMES.

### EPIG. 1.

Monſieur Domingo, is a skillfull man,
For much experience he hath lately got,
Prouing more Phiſike in an Ale-houſe Can
Then may be found in any Vintners pot,
Beere he proteſts is ſodden and refin'd,
But this he ſpeakes, being ſingle peny lin'd.

For when his purſe is ſwolne but ſixpence bigge,
Why then he ſweares; now by the Lord I thinke
All Beere in Europe is not worth aſigge:
A cup of Claret is the onely drinke,
And thus his praiſe from Beere to Wine doth go,
Euen as his Purſe in pence doth ebbe and flow.

### EPIG. 2.

Who ſeekes to pleaſe all men each way,
And not himſelfe offend :
He may begin his worke to day,
But God knowes when he'le end.

Hang

# EPIGRAMS.

### EPIG. 3. BOREAS.

Hang him bafe Gul, Ile ftab him by the Lord,
If he prefume to fpeake but halfe a word :
Ile paunch the villaine with my Rapiers point,
Or hew him with my Fauchon ioint by ioint,
Through both his cheekes my Ponniard hee fhall
Or mince pie-like Ile mangle out the flaue. (haue,
Aske who I am, you whorfon frief-gown patch?
Call me before the Conftable, or watch?
Cannot a Captaine walk in the Kings high-way?
Swouns, who do fpeak to? know ye villaines, ha?
You drūken pefants, runs your tongs on wheels?
Long you to fee your guts about your heeles?
Dooft loue me Tom? let goe my Rapier then,
Perfwade me not from killing nine or ten :
I care no more to kill them in brauado,
Then for to drinke a pipe of *Trinidado* ;
My minde to patience neuer will reftore me,
Vntill their blood do gufh in ftreams before me.
Thus doth Sir *Launcelot* in his drunken ftagger,
Sweare, curfe & raile, threatē, proteft, & fwaggers
But being next day to fober anfwer brought,
Hee's not the man can breede fo bafe a thought.

                                          **When**

# EPIGRAMS.

### EPIG. 4.

(God,
WHen *Thraso* meetes his friend, he sweares by
Vnto his chamber he shal welcome be:
Not that hee'le cloy him there with rost or sod,
Such vulgar diet with Cookes shops agree:
But hee'le present most kinde, exceeding franke,
The best *Tobacco* that he euer dranke.

Such as himselfe did make a voyage for,
And with his own hands gather'd frō the ground:
All that which others fetch he doth abhor,
His grew vpon an Iland neuer found.
Oh rare compound, a dying horse to choke,
Of English fier, and of India smoke.

### EPIG. 5.

*Diogenes* one day through *Athens* went,
With burning Torch in Sun-shine: his intent
Was (as he said) some honest man to finde:
For such were rare to meete, or he was blinde.
One late, might haue don wel like light t'haue got,
That sought his wife, met her, and knew her not:
But stay, cry mercy, she had on her maske,

How

B

# EPIGRAMS.

How could his eyes performe that spying taske?
T'is very true, t'was hard for him to doo
By Sun and Torch, let him take Lant-horne too.

### EPIG. 6.

ALas *Delfridus* keepes his bed God knowes;
Which is a signe his worship's very ill :
His griefe beyond the grounds of phisicke goes,
No Doctor that comes neare it with his skill :
Yet doth he eate drinke, talk, & sleepe profound,
Seeming to all mens iudgements healthful sound.

Then gesse the cause he thus to bed is drawne,
What, thinke you so? may such a hap procure it?
Well, faith t'is true, his hose is out at pawne,
A breechlesse chance is come he must indure it :
His Hose to Brokers Iayle committed are,
His singular and onely veluet paire.

### EPIG. 7.

SPeake Gentlemen, what shall we doe to day?
Drink some braue health vpō the dutch carous,
Or shall we to the *Globe* and see a play,
Or visit *Shore-ditch* for a bawdy-house?

Let's

# *EPIGRAMS.*

Let's call for Cardes or Dice, and haue a game;
To fit thus idle, is both finne and fhame.

This fpeakes fir *Rewill*, furnifht out with fafhion,
From difh-crownd hat, vnto the fhooes fquare toe,
That haunts a whore-houfe but for recreation,
Playes but at dice to cunny-catch, or fo;
Drinks drunke in kindnes, for good fellowfhip:
Or to the play goes but fome purfe to nip.

## EPIG. 8.

SIr Gall-Iade is a Horfe-man cu'ry day,
His Boots, and Spurs, and legs do neuer part:
He rides a horfe as paffing cleane away,
As any that goes Tiburne-ward by Cart:
Yet honeftly he payes for Hackneys hire:
But hang them Iades, he fells them when they tire.

He liues not like *Diogenes* on rootes,
But proues a mince-pie gueft vnto his Hoft:
He fcornes to walke in *Pauls* without his bootes;
And fcores his diet on the Vitlers poft:
And whe he knowes not where to haue his dinner,
He fafts, and fweares, a glutton is a finner.

B 2                    This

# *EPIGRAMS.*

### EPIG· 9. *Drude.*

THis Gentleman hath ſerued long in *France*,
  And is returned filthy full of French,
In ſingle combat being hurt by chance,
As he was cloſely foyling at a Wench :
Yet hote alarm's he hath indur'd good ſtore,
But neuer in like pockie heate before.

He had no ſooner drawne and ventred nie her,
Intending onely but to haue a bout,
When ſhe his flaske and touch-box ſet on fire;
And till this houre the burning is not out.
Iudge, was not valour in this mortall wight,
That with a ſpit-fire Serpent thus durſt fight.

### EPIG. 10. *In Meritricem.*

FAith Gentlemen you moue me to offence,
  In comming to me with vnchaſte pretence.
Haue I the lookes of a laſciuious Dame,
That you ſhould deeme me fit for wantons game?
I am not ſhe will take luſts ſinne vpon her;
Ile rather die, then dimme chaſte glorious honor.
Tempt not mine eares, an grace of Chriſt I meane
To keepe my honeſt reputation cleane.

My

# EPIGRAMS.

My hearing lets no such lewd found come in,
My fenfes loath to furfet on fweete finne.
Reuerfe your minde,that goes from grace aftray,
And God forgiue you,with my heart I pray.
The gallant notes her words,obferues her frowns
Then drawes his purfe,&lets her view his crowns,
Vowing,that if her kindnes grant him pleafure,
She fhall be Miftris to command his treafure.
The ftormes are calm'd, the guft is ouer-blowne,
And fhe replies with;*Yours,or not her owne*.
Defiring him to cenfure for the beft,
T'was but her tricke to trie if men doe ieft :
Her loue is locktwhere he may picke the truncke.
Let *Singer* iudge, if this be not a puncke.

### EPIG. 11.

G*Allus* will haue no Barber prune his beard,
Yet is his chin cleane fhauen and vnhear'd:
How comes he trimmed,you may aske me than:
His wenches doe it with their warming-pan.

### EPIG. 12.

P*Olitike Peter* meetes his friend a fhore,
That came from feas but newly tother day:

And

14

## EPIGRAMS.

And giues him French embracements by the score,
Then followes: *Dicke*, haft made good voyage, fay?
But hearing *Richards* fhares be poore and ficke:
*Peter* has hafte, and cannot drinke with *Dicke*.

Well, then he meetes an other Caueleere,
Whom he falutes about the knees and thighes,
Welcome fweete *Iames*, now by the Lord what
N'ere better *Peter*, we haue got rich prize. (cheer?
Come, come (faies *Peter*) euen a welcome quart,
For by my faith weele drinke before we part.
       *Or this,*
Faith we muft drinke, that's flat, before we part.

### EPIG. 13.

SOme doe account it golden lucke,
  They may be widdow-fped, for mucke:
Boyes on whofe chinnes no downe appeares,
Marry old Croanes of threefcore yeares:
But they are fooles to widdowes cleaue,
Let them take that which Maides doe leaue.

### EPIG. 14.

FIne *Phillip* comes into the Barbers fhop,
  Where's nitty locks muft fuffer reformation:
              **The**

# EPIGRAMS.

The chaire and cushion entertaine his slop:
The Barber craues to know his worships fashion:
His will is,shauen,for his beard is thin,
It was so lately banish'd from his chin.

But shauing oft will helpe it, he doth hope,
And therefore for the smooth face cut he calles:
Then sie, these cloathes are washt with common
Why dost thou vse such ordinary balles?    (sope,
I scorne this common trimming like a Boore:
Yet with his heart he loues a common whoore.

### EPIG. 15. *Signieur Fantasticke.*
I Scorne to meete an enemy in field,
Except he be a souldier (by this light)
I likewise scorne my reason for to yeeld;
Yea further, I doe wel nigh scorne to fight.
Moreouer,I doe scorne to be so vaine,
To draw my Rapier, and put vp againe.

I eke do scorne to walke without my man,
Yea,and I scorne good morrow and good den:
I also scorne to touch an Alehouse Can;
Thereto I scorne an ordinary queane.
Thus doth he scorne,disdainfull,proud and grim,
All but the Foole,onely he scornes not him.
Amorous

# EPIGRAMS.

### EPIG. 16.

AMorous *Auſtin* ſpends much balletting,
In riming Letters, and loue Sonnetting.
She that loues him, his Ink-horn ſhal bepaint her
And with all *Venus* titles hee'le acquaint her:
Vowing ſhe is a perfect Angell right,
When ſhe by waight is many graines too light:
Nay, all that doe but touch her with the ſtone,
Will be depos'd, that Angel ſhe is none.
How can he proue her for an Angel then,
That proues her ſelfe a diuell, tempting men,
And draweth many to the fiery pit,
Where they are burned for their entring it?
I know no cauſe wherefore he tearmes her ſo,
Vnleſſe he meanes, ſhee's one of them below,
Where *Lucifer* chiefe Prince doth domineere:
If ſhe be ſuch, then (good my harts) ſtand cleere,
Come not within the compaſſe of her ſlight,
For ſuch as doe, are haunted with a ſpright.
This Angel is not noted by her wings,
But by her taile, all full of prickes and ſtings.
And know this luſt-blind Louer's vaine is led,
To praiſe his diuel in an Angels ſted.

When

## EPIGRAMS.

### EPIG. 17.

WHen *Caualere Rake hell* is to rife
Out of his bed, he capers light and heddy :
Then wounds he fweares, you arant whore he cries,
Why what's the caufe that breakfaft is not reddy?
Can men feede like *Camelions* on the ayre?
This is the maner of his morning prayer.

Well, he fweares on vntill his breakfaft comes;
And then with teeth he falls to worke apace,
Leauing his boy a banquet all of crummes.
Difpatch you Rogue: my Rapier: that's his grace.
So forth he walkes, his ftomacke muft goe fhift,
To dine and fup abroad, by deed of guift.

### EPIG. 18.

A Wofull exclamation late I heard,
Wherewith *Tobacco* takers may be feard.
One at the point with pipe and leafe to part,
Did vow *Tobacco* worfe then Deaths blacke dart:
And prou'd it thus: you know (quoth he) my frinds
Death onely ftabbes the heart, and fo life ends:
But this fame poifon, fteeped *India* weede,
In head, hart, lungs, doth foote & cobwebs breede.
With that he gafp'd, & breath'd out fuch a fmoke,
That all the ftanders by were like to choke.

### EPIG. 19.

C *Acus* would gladly drink, but wants his purfe,
Nay, wanteth mony, which is ten times worfe
For as he vowes himfelfe, he hath not feene

C                                                    In

# *EPIGRAMS.*

In three daies space the picture of the Queene.
Yet if he meete a friend neare Tauerne signe,
Straight he intreats him take a pint of wine:
For he will giue it, that he will;no nay.
What will he giue?the other leaue to pay.
He calleth: Boy, fill vs the tother quart;
I will bestow it euen with all my hart.
Then doth he diue into his slops profound,
Where not a poore Port- cullice can be found.
Meane while his friend discharges all the wine:
Stay, stay (quoth he) or well, next shall be mine.

## EPIG. 20.

Francke in name, and Francke by nature,
Francis is a most kinde creature:
Her selfe hath suffered many a fall,
In striuing how to pleasure all.

## EPIG. 21.

Soto can proue, such as are drunke by noone,
Are long, liu'd men: the pox he can as soone.
Nay, heare his reason ere you doe condemne,
And if you finde it foolish, hisse and hem.
He saies; Good bloud is euen the life of man:
I grant him that (say you) well, go-to, than:
More drinke, the more good bloud. O thats a lie:
The more you drinke, the sooner drunke, say I.
Now he protests, you doe him mighty wrong;
Swearing a man in drinke, is three men strong:
And he will pawne his head against a penny,

One

# EPIGRAMS.

One right mad-drunk, wil brawle & fight with a-
Well, you reply; that argument is weake,    (ny.
How can a drunkard brawle, that cannot speake?
Or how can he vse weapon in his hand,
Which cannot guide his feete to goe or stand?
Hark what an oath the drunken slaue doth sweare
He is a man by that, a man may heare:
And when you see him stagger, reele, and winke,
He is a man and more; I by this drinke.

## EPIG. 22.

                                    (reeles,
WHen signieur *Sacke* & *Suger* drink-drown'd
    He vowes to hew the spurs from's fellowes
When calling for a quart of *Charnico*.    (heeles;
Into a louing league they present grow:
Then instantly vpon a cup or twaine,
Out Poniards goes, and to the stab againe.
Friends vpon that, they drinke, and so embrace:
Straight bandy daggers at each others face.
This is the humour of a mad-drunke foole,
In Tauerne pots that keeps his Fencing-schoole.

## EPIG. 23.

COrnutus was exceeding sicke and ill,
  Paind as it seemed chiefly in his hed:
He call'd his friends, meaning to make his will;
Who found him drunk, with hose & shooes abed.
To whom he said. Oh good my Maisters see,
Drinke with his dart hath all bestabbed me.
                        C 2        I here

# *EPIGRAMS.*

I here bequeath,if I doe chance to die,
To you kinde friends , & boone companions all,
A pound of good *Tobacco*, sweete and drie,
To drinke amongst you at my Funerall:
Besides, a barrell of the best strong Beere,
And Piekle-herrings, for to domineere.

### EPIG. 24.

WE men,in many faults abound;
    But two in women can be found :
The worst that from their *sexe* proceedes,
Is naught in words,and naught in deedes.

### EPIG. 25.

BId me goe sleepe? I scorne it with my heeles,
    I know my selfe as good a man as thee.
Let goe mine arme I say,leade him that reeles;
I am a right good fellow: doost thou see?
I know what longs to drinking;and I can
Abuse my selfe as well as any man.

I care no more for twenty hundred pound,
(Before the Lord)then for a very straw:
Ile fight with any he aboue the ground;
Tut,tell not me whats what,I know the law.
Rapier and dagger: hey,a kingly fight,
Ile now try falles with any,by this light.

### EPIG. 25.

BEhold,a most accomplish'd Caualeere,
    That the worlds Ape of fashions doth appeare,
                                        Wal-

# EPIGRAMS.

Walking the ſtreetes, his humours to diſcloſe,
In the French Doublet, and the Germane hoſe :
The Muffes, Cloake, Spaniſh Hat, Tolledo blade
Italian ruffe, a Shooe right Flemiſh made.
Like Lord of miſ-rule, where he comes heele reuel
And lye for wagers, with the lying'ſt diuel.

## EPIG. 27.

ASke Humors what a Feather he doth weare,
It is his humor (by the Lord) heele ſweare.
Or what he doth with ſuch a horſe-taile locke :
Or why vpon a whore he ſpends his ſtocke.
He hath a humor doth determine ſo
Why in the ſtop-throte faſhion doth he goe,
With ſcarfe about his necke, hat without band ?
It is his humor : ſweete Sir vnderſtand.
What cauſe his purſe is ſo extreame diſtreſt,
That often times tis ſcarcely penny bleſt ?
Onely a humor. If you queſtion why ?
His tongue is nere vaſurniſht with a lye.
It is his humor too he doth proteſt.
Or why with Sergants he is ſo oppreſt,
That like to ghoſts they haunt him e'rie day ?
A raſcall humor doth not loue to pay.
Obieĉt, why bootes and ſpurres are ſtill in ſeaſon?
His humor anſwers ; Humor is his reaſon.
If you perceiue his wits in wetting ſhrunke.
It commeth of a humor to be drunke.
When you behold his looks pale, thin, and poore,
Th'occaſion is, his humor, and a whoore.

C 3       And

# EPIGRAMS.

And euery thing that he doth vndertake,
It is a vaine, for fenceleffe Humors fake.

## EPIG. 28.

curfe,

THree high-way ftanders hauing cros-leffe
did greet my frind with, Sir giue vs your purfe
Though he were true man, they agreed in one,
For purfe and coine betwixt them foure was none.

## EPIG. 29.

A Gentlewoman of the dealing trade,
Procur'd her owne fweet picture to be made:
Which being done, fhe from her word did flip,
And would not pay, full due for workmanfhip.
The Painter fwore, fhe nere fhould haue it fo:
She bad him keepe it, and away did go.
He chollericke, and mighty difcontent,
Straight tooke his Penfill, and to worke he went.
Making the dog fhe held, a grim cats face,
And hung it in his fhop, to her difgrace.
Some of her friends that faw it, to her went,
In iefting manner, asking what fhe ment
To haue her picture hang where gazers fwarme,
Holding a filthy cat within her arme?
She in a fhamefull heate in hafte did hie,
The Painter to content and fatisfie:
Right glad to giue a French Crowne for his pain,
To turne her Cat into a Dog againe.

When

# *EPIGRAMS.*

### EPIG. 30.

WHen *Tarlton* clown'd it in a pleasant vaine,
    And with conceits did good opinions gaine
Vpon the stage,his merry humors shop,    (slop:
Clownes knew the Clowne by his great clownish
But now th'are gulld; for present fashion sayes,
*Dicke Tarletons* part, Gentlemens breeches playes:
In euery streete where any Gallant goes,
The swagg'ring slop, is *Tarltons* clownish hose.

### EPIG. 31. *To Lutius.*

ONe newly practiz'd in Astronomie,
    That neuer dealt in weather-wit before;
Would scrape(for sooth)acquaintance of the skie,
And by his Art, goe knocke at heauen dore.
Meane while a scholler in his studie slips,
And taught his wife skill in the Moones eclips.

Next night that friend perswades him walk alone
Into the field,to gather starres that fell,
To mix them with Philosophers rare stone,
That begets gold:he likt the motion well:
And went to watch, where stars dropt very thin,
But raine so showr'd , it wet his foole-case skin.

### EPIG. 32.                (mine eares?

WHat gallant's that whose oaths flie through
    How like a lord of *Plutoes* court he sweares:
How braue in such a bawdy-house he fought;
How rich his empty purse is outside wrought;
                                How

# *EPIGRAMS.*

How dutchman-like he swallows down his drink,
How sweete he takes *Tobacco* till he stinke:
How lofty sprited he disdaines a Boore,
How faithfull hearted he is to a (        )
How cockestaile proud he doth himselfe aduance,
How rare his spurres doe ring the morris-dance.
Now I protest by Mistris *Susans* fan.
He and his boy, will make a propper man.

## EPIG. 33.

Laugh good my Maisters if you can intend it;
For yonder comes a foole that will defend it.
Saw you a verier Asse in all your life,
That makes himselfe a pack-horse to his wife?
I would his nose where I could wish were warme,
For carrying Pearle so pretty vnder's arme.
Pearle, his wiues dog, a pretty sweet-fac'd curre,
That barkes a nights at the least fart doth sturre;
Is now not well, his cold is scarcely broke,
Therefore good husband wrap him in your cloke:
And sweet-hart, prethee helpe me to my maske;
Hold Pearle but tender, for he hath the laske:
Here, take muffe, and doe you here good man,
Now giue me Pearle, and carry you my fanne.
Alacke poore Pearle, the wretch is full of paine,
Husband take Pearle, giue me my fanne againe:
See how he quakes; faith I am like to weepe:
Come to me pearle, my scarfe good husband keep
To be with me I know my Puppy loues;
Why Pearle I say: Husband, take vp my gloues.
                                        Thus

# EPIGRAMS.

Thus goodman Idiot thinks himselfe an Earle,
That he can pleafe his wife, and carry Pearle:
But others iudge his ftate to be no higher:
Then a dogs yeoman, or fome pippin fquier.

### EPIG. 34.

WHat's he that fits and takes a nap,
Faced like the North winde of a map :
And fleeping, to the wind doth nod.
T'is *Bacchus* coofen, belly-god.

### EPIG. 35.

S*Euerus* is extreame in eloquence,
In perfum'd words, plung'd ouer head & eares,
He doth create rare phrafe, but rarer fence,
Fragments of *Latine* all about he beares.
Vnto his Seruing-man, *alias* his boy,
He vtters fpeech exceeding quaint and coy .

Deminitiue, and my defectiue flaue,
Reach my corps couerture immediately:
My pleafures pleafure is the fame to haue,
T'infconce my perfon from frigiditie.
His man beleeues all's Welch his Maifter fpoke,
Till he railes Englifh, Roague, go fetch my cloke.

### EPIG. 36.

WHy fhould the Mercers trade a fattin fute,
With Cookesgreafe be fo wickedly polute?
The reafon is, the fcandall and defame
Grew, that a greafie flouen wore the fame.

D                          An

# *EPIGRAMS.*

## EPIG. 37.

AN honeſt Vicker, and a kind conſort,
  That to the Alehouſe friendly would reſort,
To haue a game at Tables now and than,
Or drinke his pot as ſoon as any man:
As faire a gamſter, and as free from braull,
As euer man ſhall neede to play withall :
Becauſe his Hoſteſſe pledg'd him not carouſe,
Raſhly in choller did forſweare her houſe
Taking the glaſſe, this was the oath he ſwore,
Now by this drinke, Ile nere come hither more.
But mightily his Hoſteſſe did repent,
For all her gueſts to the next Alehouſe went,
Following their Vickers ſteps in euery thing,
He led the pariſh euen in a ſtring.
At length his ancient Hoſteſſe did complaine
She was vndone, vnleſſe he came againe;
Deſiring certaine friend not hers and his,
To vſe a pollicy, which ſhould be this:
Becauſe with coming he ſhould not forſwere him
To ſaue his oath, they on their backs might beare
Of this good courſe the *Vicker* wel did think, (him
And ſo they alwaies carried him to drinke,

### FINIS.

*Your Sceane is done, depart you* Epigrammes:
  *Enter Goat-footed Satyrs, but like Remmes:*
*Come humbly forth ; Why ſtand you on delay?*
  *O ho the Muſicke twang makes you ſtay.*
*Well, ſtrike it out nimbly: you ſlaues begin,*
  *For now me thinks the Fidlers hands are in.*

# SATYRS.

## SATYR. 1.

VVHo haue we here? behold him & be mute,
  Some mighty man Ile warrant by his fute.
If all the Mercers in Cheap-fide fhew fuch,
Ile giue them leaue to giue me twice as much.
I thinke the ftuffe is namelefle he doth weare:
But what fo ere it be, it is huge geare:
Marke but his gate, and giue him then his due,
Some fwaggering fellow I may fay to you.
It feemes Ambition in his big lookes fhroudes;
Some Centaure fure, begotten of the cloudes,
Now a fhame take the buzard; is it hee?
I know the ruffian, now his face I fee:
On a more gull the Sun did neuer fhine?
How with a vengeance comes the foole fo fine?
Some Noblemans caft fute is fallen vnto him;
For buying Hofe and Doublet would vndoo him.
But wot you now whither the buzard walkes?
I, into *Pauls* forfooth, and there he talkes
Of forraine tumults, vttring his aduice,
And prouing warres euen like a game at dice:
For this (faies he) as euery gamfter knowes,
Where one fide winnes, the other fide muft lofe,
Next fpeech he vtters, is his ftomacks care,
Which ordinarie yeelds the cheapeft fare:
Or if his purfe be out of tune to pay,

Then

## SATYRES.

Then he remembers tis a fasting day:
And then he talketh much against excesse,
Swearing all other Nations eate farre lesse
Then Englishmen : experience you may get
In France and Spaine:where he was neuer yet.
With a score of Figges,and halfe a pint of wine,
Some foure or fiue will very hugely dine.
Me thinks this tale is very huge in sound,
That halfe a pint should serue fiue to drink round,
And twenty figges could feede them full and fat:
But trauellers may lye?who knowes not that?
Then why not he that trauells in conceit
From east to west,when he can get no meat?
His iourney is in *Pauls* in the backe Isles,
where's stomack counts each pace a hūdred miles
A tedious thing,though chance will haue it such;
To trauell so long baitlesse,sure tis much.
Some other time,stumbling on wealthy chuffes
Worth gulling: then he swaggers all in huffes,
And tells them of a prize he was at taking,
wil be the ship-boyes childrens children making:
And that a mouse could finde no roome in hold,
It was so pestered all with pearle and gold:
Vowing to pawne his head,if it were tride,
They had more Rubies then wold paue Cheapside
A thousand other grosse and odious lies
He dares auouch,to blind dull Iudgements eyes:
Not caring what he speake,or what he sweare,
So he gaine credit at his hearers care.
Sometimes into the Royall Exchange hee'l drop,
Clad in the ruines of a Brokers shop:

And

## SATYRES.

And there his tongue runs by as on affaires,
No talke but of commodities and wares.
And what great wealth he lookes for erie wind,
Frò God knowes where, the place is hard to find.
If newes be harkened for, then he preuailes,
Setting his mint a worke to coyne false tales.
His tongs-end is betipt with forged chat,
Vttring rare lyes to be admired at:
Heele tell you of a tree that he doth know,
Vpon the which Rapiers and Daggers grow,
As good as Fleetstreet hath in any shop,
Which being ripe, downe into scabbards drop.
He hath a very peece of that same chaire,
In which *Cæsar* was stabb'd: Is it not rare?
He with his feete vpon the stones did tread,
That *Sathan* brought, & bad *Christ* make thē bread.
His wondrous trauells challenge such renowne,
That Sir *Iohn Maundiuell* is quite put downe.
Men without heads, and *Pigmies* hand-bredth hie,
Those with one leg that on their backes doe lie,
And doe the weathers iniurie disdaine,
Making their legges a penthouse for the raine,
Are tut, and tush: not any thing et all.
His knowledge knowes, what no mans notice shal
This is a mate vnmeete for euery groome,
And where he comes, peace, giue his lying roome.
He saw a Hollander in *Middleborow*,
As he was slashing of a browne laose thorow,
Whereto the hast of hunger had inclin'd him,
Cut himselfe throgh, & two that stood behind him.
Besides, he saw a fellow put to death,

*SATYRES.*

Could drinke a whole Beere barrell at a breath.
Oh this is he that will say any thing,
That to himselfe will any profit bring.
Gainst whosoere he doth speake he cares not:
For what is it that such a villaine dares not?
And though in conscience he doth not denie,
The All-commander saith, *Thou shalt not lie.*
Yet he will answer, (carelesse of soules state)
Truth-telling is a thing obtaineth hate.

### SATYR. 2.

A Man may tell his friend his fault in kindnes:
To winke at folly, is a foolish blindnes.
*God saue you Sir*; saluteth with a grace,
One he could wish neuer to see his face.
But doth not he vse meere dissimulation,
That's inside hate, and outside salutation?
Yes as I take it, yet his answer sayes,
Fashions and customes vse it now adayes.
A Gentleman perhaps may chance to meete
His Liuing-griper face to face in streete:
And though his lookes are odious vnto sight,
Yet will he doe him the French *conges* right,
And in his heart wish him as lowe as hell,
When in his words hee's glad to see him well.
Then being thus, a man may soone suppose,
There is. *God saue you Sir*, sometimes twixt foes.
Oh sir, why that's as true as you are heere,
With one example I will make it cleere:
And farre to fetch the same I will not go,
But into Houns-ditch to the Brokers row:

Or

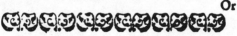

## SATYRES.

Or any place where that trade doth remaine,
Whether at Holborne Conduit, or Long-lane:
If thither you vouchsafe to turne your eye,
And see the pawnes that vnder forfait lye,
Which are forth comming sir, and safe enough,
Saies goodman Broker, in his new print ruffe:
He will not stand too strictly on a day,
Encouraging the party to delay,
With all good words the kindest may be spoke,
He turnes the Gentleman out of his cloke:
And yet betweene them both at euery meeting,
*God saue you Sir,* is their familiar greeting.
This is much kindnes sure, I pray commend him,
With great good words he highly doth defend
It is a fauour at a pinch indeed,                 (him:
A pinching friendship and a pinching deed.
The slaue may weare his suites of sattin so,
And like a man of reputation go,
When all he hath in house, or on his backe,
It is his owne by forfaitures shipwracke.
See you the brooch that long in's hat hath bin?
It may be there, it cost him not a pin:
His sundry sorts of diuers mens attire,
He weares them cheape, euen at his owne desire.
Shame ouertake the pessant for his paine,
That he should pray on losses, to his gaine:
In drawing wardrops vnder his subiection,
Being a knaue in manners and complexion:
Iumpe like to *Vsurie,* his nearest kin,
That weares a mony bag vnder his chin:
A bunch that doth resemble such a shape,

                                            And

## SATYRES.

And haired like a Parris-garden Ape,
Foaming about the chaps like some wilde Boore,
As swart and tawnie as an Indian Moore:
With narrow brow, and Squirrill eyes, he shewes,
His faces chiefest ornament is nose,
Full furnished with many a Clarret staine,
As large as any Codpiece of a Dane,
Embossed curious, euery eye doth iudge:
His Iacket faced with Moath-eaten Budge:
To which a paire of sattin sleeues he weares,
Wherein two pound of grease about he beares.
His spectacles doe in a copper case,
Hang dangling about his pissing place:
His breeches and his hose, and all the rest,
Are sutable : his gowne (I meane his hest)
Is full of threeds, intitl'd right threed bare;
But wooll thereon is wondrous scant and rare:
The welting hath him in no charges stood,
Being the ruines of a cast French-hood.
Excesse is sinfull, and he doth defie it,
A sparing whorson in attire and diet,
Onely excesse is lawfull in his chest,
For there he makes a golden Angels nest;
And vowes no farder to be found a lender,
Then that most pretious mettall doth engender:
Begetting daily more and more encrease:
His moneys slaue till wretched life surcease.
This is the *Iew* alyed very neare
Vnto the Broker: for they both doe beare
Vndoubted testimonies of their kinne:
A brace of Rascalls in a league of sinne.

Two

## SATYRES.

Two filthy Curres that will on no man fawne,
Before they taſt the ſweetneſſe of his pawne.
And then the ſlaues will be as kind forſooth,
Not as *Kind-hart*, in drawing out a tooth:
For hee doth eaſe the patient of his paine,
But they diſeaſe the borrower of his gaine.
Yet neither of them vſe extremitie,
They can be villaines euen of charitie.
To lend our Brother it is meete and fit,
Giue him roſtmeate and beate him with the ſpit
*Vſerie* ſure is requiſite and good,
And ſo is Brokeage, rightly vnderſtood:
But ſoft a litle, what is he ſayes ſo?
One of the twaine (vpon my life) I know.

## SATYRE. 3.

OH, let the Gentlewoman haue the wall,
I know her well, tis Miſtris, what d'ye call.
It woulde be ſhee both by her Mask and Fanne:
And yet it ſhould not, by her ſeruing-man;
For if mine eyes do not miſtake the foole,
He is the Vſher of ſome Dauncing Schole:
The reaſon why I do him ſuch ſuppoſe,
Is this; Mee thinkes he daunceth as he goes.
An actiue fellow, though he be but pore,
Eyther to vault vpon a horſe, or &c.
See you the huge bum Dagger at his backe,
To which no Hilt nor Iron hee doth lacke,
Oh with that blade he kepees the queanes in awe
Brauely be hacked, like a two-hand Saw,
Stamps on the ground, and byteth both his thoms
                                    Vnleſſe

E

## SATYRES.

Vnlesse he be comaunder where he comes
You damned whores, where are you? quicke cōe
Dry this *Tobacco*, Fill a dosen of beere:    )here,
Will you be brife? or long you to be hang'd?
Hold take this Match, goe light it and be hang'd.
Where stay these whores when Gent do call?
Heer's no attendaunce (by the Lord) at all.
Then downe the staires the pots in rage he throws
And in a damned vaine of swearing growes:
For he will challinge any vnder heau'n,
To sweare with him, and giue him sixe at seuen.
Oh, he is an accomplish'd Gentleman,
And many rare conceited knackes he can:
Which yeld to him a greater store of gaine,
Then iuggling *Kinges*, hey Passe ledgerdemaine?
His witt's his lyuing: one of quaint deuice,
For Bowling-allies. Cockpits, Cards, or Dice,
To those exployts he euer stands prepar'd:
A Villaine excellent at a Bum card.
The Knaue of Clubbes he any time can burne,
And finde him in his bosome, for his turne.
Tut, he hath Cards for any kind of game,
*Primero, Saunt*, or what soeuer name:
Make him but dealer, all his fellowes sweares
If you doe finde good dealing, take his eares.
But come to Dice: why thats his only trade,
*Michell Mum-chaunce* his owne invention made.
He hath a stocke whereon his liuing stayes,
And they are *Fullams* and *Bardquarter-trayes*:
His *Langrets*, with his *Hie men*, and his *low*,
Are ready what his pleasure is to throw.

                                           His

## SATYRES.

His ſtopt Dice with Quick-ſiluer neuer miſſe.
He calles for come on fiue, and there it is:
Or elſe heele haue it with fiue and a reach,
Although it coſt his neck the Halter ſtreach.
Beſides all this ſame kinde of cheating art,
The Gentleman hath ſome good other part,
well ſeene in *Magicke* and *Aſtrologie*,
Flinging a figuer woundrous handſomlie:
Which if it doth not miſſe, it ſure doth hit.
Of troth the man hath great ſtore of ſmall wit.
And note him whetherſoeuer he goes,
His booke of Characters is in his hoſe.
His dinner he will not perſume to take,
Ere he aske counſell of Almanacke.
Heele finde if one proue falſe vnto his wiſe,
Onelie with Oxe blood and a ruſtie knife.
He can transforme himſelfe vnto an Aſſe,
Shew you the Diuell in a Chriſtall glaſſe:
The Diuell ſay you? why I, is that ſuch wonder?
Being conſortes, they will not be a ſunder.
*Alcumie* in his braines ſo ſure doth ſettle,
He can make golde of any copper ket'le;
With in a three weekes ſpace, or ſuch a thing,
Riches vpon the whole world he could bring;
But in his one purſe one ſhall hardly ſpie it,
Witneſſe his Hoſteſſe, for a twelue-months diet:
Who would be glad of gold or ſiluer neither.
But ſweares by chalke, & poſt, ſhe can get neither.
More, he will teach any to gaine there loue,
As thus (ſaies he) Take me a turtle Doue,
And in an Ouen let her lye and bake

E 2                                    So

### SATYRES.

So dry that you may powder of her make:
Which being put into a cup of vine,
The wench that drinks it will to loue incline:
And shall not sleepe in quiet in her bed
Till she be eased of her maiden-head.
This is *probatum*, and it hath bin tride,
Or else the Cunning-man cunningly lide:
It may be so, a lye is not so strange,
Perhaps he spake it when the Moone did change:
And thereupon no doubt th'occasion sprung,
Vnconstant *Luna* ouer-rul'd his tongue.
*Astrenomers* that traffique with the skie,
By common censure sometime meete the lie:
Although indeede their blame is not so much.
When Stars and Planets faile, and keep not tutch,
And so this fellow with his large profession,
That ends his triall in a faire digression:
*Philosophers* bequeashed him then stone,
To make gold with, yet can his purse hold none.

### SATYR. 4.

MElliuuius sweete Rose-watred eloquence,
Thou that hast hunted Barbarisme hence,
And taught the Goodman *Cobbin* at his Plow,
To be as eloquent as *Tullie* now :
Who nominates his bread and cheese a name,
(That doth vntrusse the nature of the same)
*His stomacke stayer.* How doe like the phrase?
Are Plough-men simple fellowes nowadaies?
Not so my Maisters : what meanes *Singer* then
And *Pope* the Clowne, to speake so Boorish, when
They

## SATYRES.

They counterfait the Clownes vpon the Stage?
Since Country fellowes grow in this same age
To be so quaint in their new printed speech,
That cloth will now compare with Veluet breech
Let him discourse euen where and when he dare,
Talke nere so Inkhorne, learnedly, and rare,
Sweare, Cloth breech is a pessant (by the Lord)
Threaten to draw his (wrath-venger) his sword:
Tush, Cloth-breech doth deride him with a laugh,
And lets him see *Bune-baster*, thats his staffe:
Then tels him brother, friend, or so forth, heare ye,
Tis not your Knitting-needle makes me feare ye,
If to ascention you are so declinde,
I haue a restitution in my minde:
For though your beard do stand so fine mustated,
Perhaps your nose may be transfisticated.
Man, I dare challenge thee to throw the sledge,
To iumpe or leape-ouer a ditch or hedge,
To wrastle, play at stoole ball, or to runne,
To pitch the barre, or to shoote off a gunne.
To play at loggets, nine-holes, or ten-pinnes,
To try it out at foote-ball by the shinnes:
At tichtacke, Irish, noddy, maw, and ruffe,
At hot-cockles, leap-frog, or blindman-buffe,
To drinke halfe pots, or deale at the whole can,
To play at base, or pen and ink-horne, sir Ihan,
To dance the morris, play at barly-breake,
At all exploits a man can thinke or speake,
At shoue-groat, venter point, or crosse and pile,
At beshrew him thats last at yonder stile,
At leaping ore a midsommer bone-fier,

E 3                              Or

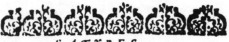

## SATYRES.

Or at the drawing Dun out of the myer :
At any of these, or all these presently,
Wag but your finger, I am for you, I.
I scorne(that am a youngster of our towne)
To let a Bow-bell cockney put me downe.
This is a gallant farre beyond a gull,
For very valour fills his pockets full.
wit showers vpon him wisedomes raine in plenty,
For heele be hang'd, if any man finde twenty
In all their parish, whatsoere they be,
Can shew a head so pollitike as he.
It was his fathers lucke of late to die
*Vntestate*; he about the Legacie
To London came, inquiring all about,
How he might finde a Ciuil-villaine out :
Being vnto a Ciuill-lawyer sent,
Pray sir(quoth he) ase you the man I meant,
That haue a certaine kinde of occupation,
About dead men that leaue things out of fashion :
Death hath done that which t'answer he's not able
My father he is dyed destable :
I being his eldest heire, he did prefer
Me sir, to be his executioner :
And very briefly my request to finish,
Pray how may I by law, his goods diminish.
Was this a Clowne? tell true, or was a none?
You make fat Clownes, if such as he be one :
A man may sweare, if he were vrg'd to it,
Foolisher fellowes, haue not so much wit.
Oh such as he, are euen the onely men,
Loue-letters in a Milke-maides praise to pen:

Lines

## SATYRES.

Lines that will worke the curstest sullen shrow,
To loue a man whether she will or no.
Being most wonderous patheticall,
To make *Sisse* out a cry in loue withall:
He scornes that master schoolmaister should think
He wants his ayde in halfe a pen of incke :
All that he doth, it commeth euery whit
From Natures dry-fat, his owne mother wit.
*Or thus:*
Thou honysuckle of the hawthorne hedge,
Vouchsafe in *Cupids* cup my heart to pledge :
My hearts deare blood sweete *Sisse*, is thy carouse
Worth all the Ale in gammer *Gubbins* house ?
I say no more, affaires call me away,
My fathers horse for prouender doth stay.
Be thou the Lady *ressu light* to me,
Sir *Trollololle* I will proue to thee.
Written in haste : farewell my Cowslippe sweete,
Pray lets a Sunday at the Ale-house meete.

## SATYR. 5.

TIs a bad world, the common speech doth go,
    And he complaines that helpes to make it so:
Yet euery man th'imputed crime would shunne,
Hypocrisie with a fine threed is spunne.
Each striues to shew the very best in seeming,
Honest enough, if honest in esteeming,
Praise waites vpon him now with much renowne,
That wraps vp vices vnder Vertues gowne:
Commending with good words religious deedes,
To helpe the poore, supply our neighbours needs:
                                                Do

## SATYRES.

Do no man wrong, giue euery man his owne,
Be friend to all, and enemie to none,
Haue charitie, auoid contentious strife.
Oft he speakes thus, that nere did good in's life.
*Derision* hath an ore in euery boate,
In's neighbours eye he quickely spies a moate:
But the great beame thats noted in his own,
He lets remaine, and neuer thinks thereon.
Some doe report he beares about a sacke,
Halfe hanging forwards, halfe behinde at's backe,
And his owne faults, (quite out of sight & minde)
He casts into the part that hangs behinde:
But other mens he putteth in before,
And into them he looketh euermore.
*Contempt* comes very neare to th'others vaine,
He hates all good deserts with proud disdaine.
*Rashnesse* is his continuall walking mate,
Costly appareld, loftie in his gate:
Vp to the eares in double ruffes and starch,
God blesse your eysight when you see him march
Statutes and lawes, he dare presume to breake,
Against superiors cares not what he speake.
It is his humors recreation fits,
To beate Constables, and resist all writs:
Swearing, the ripest wits are childish young,
Vnlesse they gaine instructions from his tongue.
Theres nothing done amongst the very best,
But hee'le deride it with some bitter iest.
It's meate and drinke vnto him alwaies, when
He may be censuring of other men.
If a man doe but toward a Tauerne looke,

He

## SATYRES.

He is a drunkard hee'le sweare on a booke:
Or if one part a fray of good intention,
He is a quarreller, and loues dissention.
Those that with silence vaine discourses breake,
Are proud fantastickes, that disdaine to speake.
Such as speake soberly with wisedomes leasure,
Are fooles, that in affected speech take pleasure.
If he heare any that reproueth vice,
He saies, theres none but hypocrites so nice.
No honest woman that can passe along,
But must endure some scandall from his tongue.
She deales crosse blowes her husband neuer feeles,
This Gentlewoman weareth capering heeles.
There minces *Mall*, to see what youth will like her,
Her eyes doe beare her witnes shee's a striker.
Wonders, a wench new dipt in beauties blaze,
She is a maide, as maides go nowadaies.
And thus *Contempt* makes choysest recreation,
In holding euery one in detestation:
His common gate is of the ietting size,
He hath a paire of euer-staring eyes,
And lookes a man so hungry in the face,
As he would eate him vp, and nere say grace.
A little low crownd hat he alwaies weares,
And fore-horse like therein a feather beares:
Goodly curld lockes, but surely tis great pitty,
For want of kembing they are beastly nitty.
His doublet is a cut cast sattin one,
He scorns to buy new now, that nere bought none
Spotted in diuers places with pure fat:
Knowne for a right tall trencher-man by that.

F                                        His

## SATYRES.

His breeches that came to him by befrending,
Are desperate like himselfe, & quite past mending
He takes a common course to goe vntrust,
Except his shirt's a washing; then he must
Goe woollward for the time: he scornes it he,
That worth two shirts his Laundresse should him
The weapons that his humors doe afford,    (see.
Is bum-dagger, and basket-hilted swoard:
And these in euery Bawdy house are drawne
Twice in a day, vnlesse they be at pawne.
If any fall together by the eares,
To field cries he, why zownes (to field) he sweares
Shew your selues men: hey, slash it out with blowes
Let one make tothers gut garter his hose:
Make steele and yron vmpires to the fray,
You shall haue me goe with, to see faire play:
Let me alone, for I will haue a care
To see that one doe kill the other faire,
This is *Contempt*, thats euery ones disdainer,
The strife pursuer, and the peace refrainer:
*Hates* thunderbolt, damn'd : *Murders* larum-bell,
A neare deare kinsman to the diuell of hell:
And he whom Sathan to his humor brings,
Is th'only man for all detested things.

### SATYR. 6.

Tom's no good fellow, nor no honest man:
  Hang him, he would not pledge *Raph* halfe a
But if a friend may speak as he doth thinke, (can:
*Will* is a right good fellow by this drinke.
Oh *William, William*, th'art as kinde a youth
As euer I was drunke with, thats the trueth.

                                          *Tom*

## SATYRES.

*Tom* is no more like thee then chalk's like cheefe,
To pledge a health, or to drinke vp se freese:
Fill him his beaker, he will neuer flinch,
To giue a full quart pot the empty pinch.
Hee'le looke vnto your water well enough,
And hath an eye that no man leaues a snuffe :
A pox of peece-meale drinking (*William* saies)
Play it away, weele haue no stops and staies :
Blowne drinke is odious, what man can difgeft it?
No faithfull drunkard but he doth deteft it.
I hate halfe this; out with it, and an end,
He is a buzard will not pledge his friend,  (clofed
But ftands as though his drinkes malt-facke were
With, *Here's t'yee Sir againft you are difpofed* ?
How fay my friend, and may I be fo bold?
Blowing on's beere like broth, to make it cold,
Keeping the full glaffe till it ftand and fower
Drinking but halfe a mile an hower:
Vnworthy to make one, or gaine a place,
Where boone companions gage the pots apace.
A mans a man, and therewithall an end,
Good fellowfhip was bred and borne to fpend:
No man ere faw a pound of forrow yet,
Could be alowd to pay an ounce of debt.
We may be here to day, and gone to morrow,
Call me for fix pots more, come on, hang forrow,
Tut, lacke an other day, why tis all one,
When we are dead, then all the world is gone.
Begin to me good *Ned*, what, haft gone right?
Is it the fame that tickled me laft night?
We gaue the Brewers diet-drinke a wipe,

F 2                                    Braue

## SATYRES.

Braue Malt-Tobacco in a quart pot pipe:
It netled me, and did my braines infpire:
I haue forfworne your drinking fmoke and fier:
Out vpon Cane and leafe Tobacco fmell,
Diuells take home your drinke, keepe it in hell.
Carowfe in Canon *Trinidado* fmoake,
Drinke healths to one an other till you choake,
And let the *Indians* pledge you till they fweate,
Giue me the element that drowneth heate:
Strong fodden water is a vertuous thing,
It makes one fweare and fwagger like a King,
And hath more hidden vertue then you thinke:
For Ile maintaine, good liquor's meate and drink:
Nay, Ile goe further with you, for in troth
It is as good as meate, and drinke, and cloth:
For he that is in Malt-mans Hall inrolde,
Cares not a point for hunger nor for colde.
If he be cold, he drinketh till he fweate,
If he be hot, he drinkes to lay the heate:
So that how ere it be, cold or hot,
To precious vfe he doth apply the pot:
And will approue it phifically found,
If it be drunke vpon the *Danifh* round,
Or taken with a pickle-herring or two,
As Flemmings at Saint *Katherines* vfe to do:
Which fifh hath vertue eaten falt and raw,
To pull drinke to it, euen as leate doth ftraw.
Oh tis a very whetftone to the braine,
A March-beere fhewer puts downe Aprill raine;
It makes a man actiue to leape and fpring,
To dance and vault, to carowle and to fing.

For

## SATYRES.

For all exploits it doth a man enable,
T'out leape mens heads, and caper ore the table:
To burne facke with a candle till he reeles,
And then to trip vp his companions heeles ɩ
To fing like the great Organ-pipe in *Poules*,
And cenfure all men vnder his controules:
Againſt all commers ready to maintaine,
That deepeſt wit is in a drunken braine.
I marry is it, that it is he knowes it,
And by this drinke, at all times will depofe it.
He fayes, that day is to a minute fhrunke,
In which he makes not fome good fellow drunke:
As for nine worthies on his Hoſtes wall,
He knowes three worthy drunkards paſſe them all
The firſt of them in many a Tauerne tride,
At laſt fubdued by *Aquauita*, dide.
His fecond Worthies date was brought to fine,
Feaſting with Oyſters and braue Reniſh wine.
The third, whom diuers Dutch men held ful deare
Was ſtabb'd by pickeld herrings & ſtrong beere:
Well, happy is the man doth rightly know,
The vertue of three cups of *Charnice*,
Being taken faſting, th'onely cure for fleam,
It worketh wonders on the braine, extreame
A pottle of wine at morning, or at night,
Drunke with an apple, is employed right,
To rince the Liuer, and to purifie
A dead ſicke heart from all infirmitie.

### SATYR. 7

Liu'd the Philofopher *Heraclitus*
In *Troynouant*, as once in *Ephefus*.

We re

## SATYRES.

Were not *Democrites* liue,s-date full done,
But he with vs an's glasse some sand to runne?
How would the first,dry-weepe his watry eyes?
And th'others laughter eccho through the skies?
For while they in this world were resident,
*Heraclitus* for vertues banishment,
Perform'd a pensiue teare-complaining part:
*Democrates*, he laugh'd euen from his hart,
Spending his time in a continuall iest,
To see base *Vice* so highly in request.
Weepe *Vertues* want,and giue sad sighes to boote:
*Vice* rides on horsedacke,*Vertue* goes on foote:
Yet laugh againe as fast on'th'others side,
To see so vile a scumme prefer'd to ride.
But what wilt helpe to sigh on flinty sin?
T'will not be mollifide as it hath bin :
T is farre more highly fauour'd then before,
Sin's no beggar standing at the dore,
That by his patches doth his want dispute,
But a right welcome Sir,for's costly sute :
And maske about with such an ostentation:
World saies;*Vice*-haters loues no recreation.
You shall haue smooth-fac'd neate dissimulation,
A true *What lacke ye?* by his occupation:
Will(*I in trueth,yes truely*) shew you ware,
All London cannot with his stuffe compare:
Nay,if you match it(go from him to any)
Take his for nothing,pay him not a penny.
At this,my simple honest Country-man
Takes *Trueth* and *Truely* for a Puritan;
And dares in's conscience sweare he loues no lying
                                                But

### SATYRES.

But that they deale for, he giues him the buying.
To let him haue a peniworth he is willing,
Yet for a groates worth makes him pay a shilling;
Giues goodman *Trollop* one thing for an other,
And saies, hee'le vse him as he were his brother :
But while his eares with brothers tearms he feeds,
He proueth but    Coosen in his deedes :
Brotherhood once in kindred bore the sway,
But that dates out, and Coosnage hath the day.
The foregone ages that are spent and donne,
The old time past, that calls time present, Sonne;
Saw better years, & more plaine meaning howers
Then presently, or future following ours.
The world is naught, and now vpon the ending,
Grows worse & worse, & fardest off frō mending.
Seuen grand diuels, bred and borne in hell,
Are grac'd like Monarchs on the earth to dwell:
where they comand the worlds whole globy roūd
Leauing poore *Vertuous* life no dwelling ground.
*Pride* is the first, and he began with *Eue*,
Whose cognisance still's worne on womens sleeue
He fits the humors of them in their kinde,
With euery moneth, new liueries to their minde:
A buske, a maske, a fanne, a monstrous ruffe,
A boulster for their buttockes, and such stuffe:
More light &toyish then the wind blowne chaffe
As though they meant to make the diuell laste.
The next that marcheth is the roote of euill,
Call'd *Couetousnesse*, a greedy rascall deuill:
To fill old yron barred chests, he rakes,
great rents for little Cottages he takes :
Hordeth vp corne, in hope to haue a yeere,

## SATYRES.

Fit for his cut-throat humor, to fell deere.
Then is there a notorious bawdy feend,
Nam'd *Lecherie*, who all his time doth spend
In two wheeld Coach, and bafon occupation:
Making a vaulting houfe his recreation,
Vnto his doore in fummer howerly marches,
And euery Tearme looke for him in the Arches.
*Ennie's* the fourth, a Diuell dogged fprighted;
In others harmes he chiefly is delighted:
His heart againft all charity is fteeld,
His frownes are all challenges to the field:
Though nothing croffe him, yet he murmers euer
He laughes at fome mans loffe, or els laughs neuer.
*Wrath* is the next, that fwaggers, fights, & fweares,
In Fleetftreete brauely at it by the eares:
Parboild in rage, pepperd in heate of fire,
Hot liuerd, and as chollericke as fire.
Vitlers and Sergants are beholden to him,
Till halter deftenie, of life vndo him.
Sixe lubberly gor-belled deuill great,
Is *Gluttony*, fwolne with exceffe of meate:
His bellifhip containes th'infatiate gut,
Paunch'd liquor proofe, an'twere a Malmfie-but,
Dulled with drinke: this is his vfuall phraife,
Yet one quart, and a morfell more, he faies.
The laft is *Sloth*, a lazie diuelifh cur,
So truft in *Idleneffe*, he fcarce can ftur:
Lumpifh and heauy thoughts, of Sathans giuing,
That rather begs, then labours for his liuing.
Thefe feuen are feends come forth of Hells darke
On earth feducing foules, mifguiding men. (den,

### FINIS.

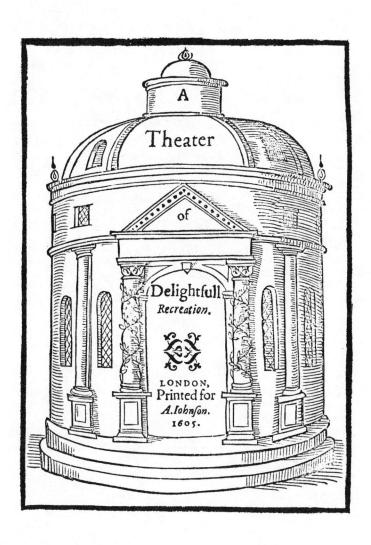

A

Theater

of

Delightfull
*Recreation.*

LONDON,
Printed for
A. Iohnson.
1605.

# TO THE WEL-
## AFFECTED READER.

*Etire thy lookes, and view with Iudgements eyes*
*Mens vaine delights, that paſſe in poſting wiſe,*
*Their liking firſt, and their diſlike ſucceeding,*
*Their euery pleaſure, ſome diſpleaſure breeding:*
*How out of league with all things lou'd they fall,*
*How all their glory is* Times tennis-ball:
*And this compar'd, fixe* Vertue *in thy mind,*
*Which is moſt ſtayd, and heauen bred by kind.*
*No calling backe of nimble light-foote* Time,
*But to repent, is to vnwrite vaine rime.*
*What worſer paines can any Poet take,*
*Then rime himſelfe to death for* Venus ſake?
*No minute more to* Satyrs *I will lend,*
*Nor drop of inke on* Epigram *Ile ſpend:*
*Let Humoriſts do as themſelues thinke good,*
*My pen hath done with* Letting Humors *blood:*
*Ile ſhow no more to each fantaſtique aſſe*
*His pourtraiture in* Humors Looking-glaſſe.

*Scatter your abſurd follies as tofore,*
*I am reſolu'd to gather them no more.*
Deaths Challenge, *with* Ile ſtab, *has paſs'd the Preſſe,*
*And ſo I leaue him to his powerfulneſſe:*
*With* Hell broke looſe *I haue no more to doo,*
Leyden *is hang'd and* Knipperdulling *too.*
*My idle houres to theſe I did allow,*
*But better buſineſſe I haue for them now.*
*And all the leiſure Poetrie can get,*
*Shall pay ſuch lines as are in* Vertues *debt:*
*For verſe ill vs'd, and precious time miſ-ſpent,*
*Poets conuert, be truly penitent.*

S. R.

# To all prophane Poets, wearing
## VENVS wanton Liuerie, with
### *Cupids* blind cogniſance.

*I*Dle good-wits that turne the glaſſe of Time
  *To runne for vanitie each ſingle ſand,*
   *Compoſing volumes full of wanton rime,*
*Fables of* Cupid *all you take in hand,*
    *Great are your workes, and yet the goodneſſe ſmall,*
    *For Beauties lightneſſe is the worth of all.*

*Sup-*

Suppofedly you raife them to the skies,
Whom you with pen bepaint about the face,
And by the whole fale vtter louers lies,
Yet done (as you imagine) with great grace.
　　But how can grace concurre with fuch an euill,
　　Since he that praifeth pride, commends the deuill?

Your graces in this veine no further goes,
But to be counted fine conceited liers,
That commendations all wife men beftowes,
Worthleffe defert a worthleffe meede requiers:
　　Your labor's loft, your time's as vainely fpent,
　　Twas errors crooked way Inuention went.

One writes a Sonnet of his miftres fan,
Bleßing the bird that did the feathers beare:
Another fhewes himfelfe as wife a man
To rime vpon the fhoo ftrings fhe doth weare,
　　And of her bodkin, fcarfe, and paire of gloues,
　　And little dog that fhe fo kindly loues.

Another tels the actions of the gods,
Their heady riots and outragious ftrife,
How they haue bene amongft themfelues at ods
About the faireneffe of blacke Vulcans wife:
　　And then what cruelties her fonne did fhow,
　　That wants a paire of eyes to guide his bow.

*Oh sacred Muses, you may iust complaine*
*Against those heau'nly sparkes of wit you nourish,*
*Who their best faculties so much prophane,*
*Which should in euery good endeuour flourish:*
    *For those which greatest gifts do that way ow,*
    *Do euen the worst and basest things bestow.*

*How miserable wit's employd, who sees not?*
*Spent prodigall, in praising* Venus *pride,*
*In such sort as with Vertue it agrees not,*
*On them haue nought praise-worthy on their side:*
    *Diuinest arts thereby sustaine abuses,*
    *Which were ordain'd for sanctified vses.*

*Vnto renowned* Vertue *proue more kind,*
*Your gifts vnto her seruice dedicate,*
*And the reward of Honor you shall find,*
*When Beautie shall lie rotting out of date,*
    *Blasted by death, a stinking vnder ground,*
    *Consum'd in graue, and neuer to be found.*

                   S. R.

**To**

# To his louing friend Mr. S. R.

VAnish things worthlesse, from Inuention flie,
 You now mistake, not as I was am I,
It is a simple thing, most childish base,
To be a Poet for a womans face:
I held an heresie, and here recant,
My pen for euer womens pride shall want,
Except their beautie and their faire proceeds
From vertuous, chast, and ciuill modest deeds.
This is an argument, that fooles they bee,
Men flattring them so grosse, they cannot see:
But euen as fops composed all of pride,
Still loue them most which haue them most belide.
Vnto such diuels I held a candle late,
But now, kind friend, I will thee imitate,
My Poetrie Ile in a new mould cast,
Verse shall do penance for my follies past.

E. P.

# To the Muses.

CAlliope, diuine and heauenly Muse,
 With all thy sisters on the sacred Mount,
Whom the best spirits do for nurses chuse,

*Hauing*

*Hauing you all in reuerent account:*
    *Receiue the Laurell which our Mufe refignes,*
    *True penitent for idle paffed lines.*

*Grace not the gracele∬e Poets of our time,*
*That vfe you but to ferue their needy ftates,*
*Such as for dayly profit hackney rime:*
*Thofe* Venus *brokers, and loues-fhifting mates,*
    *That fell you all, to buy themfelues their dinner,*
    *Famifh the flaues, and make their cheekes looke thinner.*

*Extend your bountie vnto free borne fpirits,*
*That imitate your felues (for you are free)*
*Let them receiue their well-deferuing merits,*
*And to* Parnaffus *euer welcome bee:*
    *For they do fcorne to lay you out to pawne,*
    *Like fuch as do on Lords and Ladies fawne.*

## To his conftant beloued friend Mr. S.R.

*THy Theater is built of curious frame,*
    *And fixt as firme vpon a fure foundation,*
*All thofe whofe eyes fhall entertaine the fame,*
*Muft come to fee diuineft Recreation.*
    *There's no prophane∬e in this worke difclofed,*
    *But as the name imports it is compofed.*

                                                    *All*

*All is true action that's presented here,*
*And every actor credit with him brings:*
*Vpon this stage great monarches do appeare,*
*Strong* Samson *steps with bloudy wounded Kings:*
*Some blest by God, some curst when he forsooke them,*
*As from truths register the author tooke them.*

R. W.

## To his louing and no lesse beloued friend
### M. Sam. Rowlands.

*T*He world commends each toy,
   *And entertaines it gladly.*
*What vanitie, but this our age*
*Pursues it strange and madly?*
*Things worthlesse much esteemd,*
*The worthfull most despisde,*
*And vertue dayly counterfait,*
*Vice cunningly disguisde.*
*This makes me, when into*
*Thy Theater I looke,*
*To hold thee happy, leauing toyes,*
*To write so good a booke.*

I. G.

B             To

# To Time.

THou great confumer of huge monuments,
  That mak'ſt ſtiffe Marble turne to cindry duſt:
Kingdomes ſubuerter, whom no power preuents,
With canker fretting braſſe, iron with ruſt.
  Thou that didſt bring the pow'rfull Monarchies
To their full height, then ouerthrewſt their pride:
Thou that the arched Ilion didſt ſurpriſe,
Whoſe townes with ten yeares ſuccors were ſupplide.
  That in the boſome of fore paſſed age
The fruit of many a noble Muſe haſt found,
And kept till now, in ſcorne of enuies rage,
When in obliuions gulfe great Kings were drownd:
  Do thou preſerue this worke vntill that day,
  When earth ſhall melt, the vniuerſe decay.

                              Tho. Andrew.


                    ADAMS

# ADAMS PASSION
## VPON HIS FALL.

OFfpring of earth, my ill condition'd race,
With forrow looke vpon your parents cafe,
That by his finne brought death vnto you all,
For you haue deadly intereſt in my fall.
I in whoſe foule perfection made abode,
I that was like my all-creating God,
I being endude with admirable feature,
I that had Lordly rule of euery creature;
Oh I to whom all graces did abound,
Of all God made, am moſt ingratefull found.
Come wofull *Eue*, as I fhar'd finne with thee,
Bring euery teare thou haſt and mourne with mee:
I tooke the fruite with thee that brought thefe feares,
Do thou take woe with me, oh ioyne in teares.
We that in grace and glory late haue bin,
Are falne from God by diſobedient fin.
Weepe thou for hearkning what the Serpent ſayd,
And I will weepe for being both betrayd:
Weepe thou for yeelding firſt to his perſwaſion,
And I will weepe for giuing me occaſion:

B 2                    Let

Let both our soules with sorrow be repleate,
Because we both haue bene seduc'd to eate.
When in the coole of day Gods voice I heard,
O how my senses trembled! then I feard,
And sought to hide me from his angry face,
(Foole as I was, he sees in eu'ry place)
Where art thou *Adam*, said he? that *where art*
Was euen a hell of horror to my hart:
With fig-leaues wrapt, I to the Lord replide,
For shame of nakednesse I do me hide.
Who told thee of thy nakednes, said hee?
Hast thou not eate of the forbidden tree,
Concerning which, I said thou shouldest not?
Then for my selfe this bad excuse I got,
The woman that thou gau'st with me to liue,
Why she did of that fruite vnto me giue.
Then (said he) Woman, why hast thou done this?
She said, The Serpent caus'd me do amisse.
But these excuses no way could vs free,
Gods curses were ponounc'd against all three:
Yea euen the earth was cursed for my sake,
And I enioyned paines therewith to take,
By toylsome labour, and in weary sweate,
To make my hands the earners of my meate.
Then did my dreadfull sin-incensed Lord,
Appoint a Cherubin with fiery sword,
To keepe the passage to the tree of life,

Driuing

Driuing me forth of *Eden* with my wife,
Death at my heeles,and Miſery beſide me,
My enemy the Diuell to deride me.
Cloath'd with a leather coate of dead beaſts skins,
Which garment made me mindfull of my ſins:
And the reward due to me for the ſame,
My outſide death,my inſide ſinne and ſhame.
Now ſeruile labour for my ſelfe I found,
I got a ſpade,and fell to dig the ground:
For from earths bountie nothing I could gaine,
Vnleſſe I bought it with the price of paine.
If I in Paradiſe had neuer bin,
Farre leſſe perplexitie I ſhould be in,
My doubts,and feares,and all my ſorrowes grow,
That I true happineſſe did taſt and know.
To ſay,*I had,* to thinke,*If I had knowne,*
Are of themſelues torments enough alone.
Yet hope encounters comfort by the way,
Iehouah to the Serpent thus did ſay,
Betwixt you ſhall an enmitie be bred,
The womans ſeed ſhall breake the Serpents head.
This confidence preuents hels friend *Deſpaire,*
A ſecond *Adam* ſhall with grace repaire
The ruines that the firſt hath ſinfull made:
On this foundation let the faith be laid
Of all my offspring:ſinne from me enſude,
Sinne,death and hell by him ſhall be ſubdude.

When man was ouercome by Sathans euill,
He loft the Paradice where he was placed;
When man by grace fhall ouercome the diuell,
He fhall gaine heauen, whence that fiend was chafed:
   He conquering vs, did caufe Gods wrath increafe;
   We conquering him, with God fhall be at peace.

# Caines horror of minde for the in-
## humane murder of his Brother.

BEhold the wretched heire of all the earth,
Moft gracel效e man, bloudy accurfed *Caine*,
The firft that in this world hath had his birth,
The worft that euer fhall be borne againe,
   In confcience fo tormented and diftreft,
   I haue not one calme thought of quiet reft.

If wofull *Adam* when he fell from grace,
In fuch a feare of his tranfgreffion ftood,
That he did hide him from *Iehouahs* face,
What fhall I do, being all imbrude in blood?
   Whofe blood? *My brothers:* what? a wicked man?
   Oh no, moft iuft, my confcience witneffe can.

I

I did prefent the Lord with my oblation,
My brother offered vp his facrifice,
And that of his was held in eftimation,
Mine nothing fet by in th'Almighties eyes,
    Whereat affection from him I eftranged,
    And vnto wrath my countenance I changed.

Why art thou angry? faid the Lord to me,
Why doth thy lookes feeme other then to fore?
If thou do well, it will returne to thee,
If thou do ill, finne lieth at the dore.
    Vnto dominion and to rule afpire,
    And *Abel* fhall incline to thy defire.

But what he fpake, my heart regarded not,
Wrath ftopt mine eares, and would not let me heare.
For when my brother in the field I got,
I lifted vp my hand againft him there,
    And that fame ftroke which did his life controule,
    Kild him a body, and my felfe a foule.

What heard I then? oh this: *Caine*, Where's thy brother?
When defp'rate wretch I did this anfwer make,
Am I his keeper? do we gard each other?
What charge do we of one another take?
    *What haft thou done?* faid God, *thy deed is found,*
    *For Abels blood cries vengeance from the ground.*

                                Euen

Euen from the earth thou art accurſed now,
Whoſe mouth receiu'd the blood thy hand hath ſhed,
No profit,though thou till,ſhall it allow,
The ſtrength of it ſhall from thy vſe be fled.
    Be thou a vagabond and fugitiue,
    That neuer ſhalt in any action thriue.

Then in the horror of my ſoule I ſpake,
As deſp'rate moſt vnworthy wretch to liue,
(No ſute of mercy purpoſing to make)
*My ſinne is greater then thou canſt forgiue*:
    Nothing but vengeance I expect to find,
    For there's no roome for ſorrow in my mind.

Behold this day I am an outcaſt made,
And from the vpper face of th'earth I go:
Thy countenance thou likewiſe haſt denaid,
One looke of fauour neuer to beſtow.
    And whoſoeuer findes me out, he will
    Euen murder me,as I did *Abel* kill.

Feare,and Deſpaire,and I, all three in one,
My wofull heart do into ſhares deuide,
But greedy Feare would haue it all alone,
Till I and blacke Deſpaire grew ſtronger ſide,
    And then we two together did incline,
    That all my heart ſhould be Deſpaires and mine.
                        **And**

And now I do all that Defpaire would haue me,
Being refolute refolu'd on euill thus,
For my iniquitie God cannot faue me,
There is no grace that can do good for vs:
    Leade on Defpaire, with finne I will go hide me,
    Gods iuftice comes, his grace can nere abide me.

# The dreadfull burning of
## *finfull Sodome.*

IT was about meridian of the day,
  (When *Phœbus* in his height of burning fway,
  Did like vnto a giant runne his race,
About the fpheare of his celeftiall place)
That *Abraham* the bleffed man of God,
At his tent doore for his repofe abode,
Where lifting vp his eyes, behold, ftood three
Of Angels nature, feeming men to bee.
With reuerence he bowed to the ground,
And faid, my Lord, if I haue fauour found,
Paffe not away, but here refrefh with mee
Vnder the fhadow of this pleafant tree,
Then prefently with greateft fpeed he went
To vertuous *Sara* being in the tent,

      C            And

And will'd her make some cakes of finest meale,
Feasting themselues with butter, milke, and veale
Vnder the arbors coole delightfull leaues,
Where he the promise of a sonne receiues.
Then rising thence, to Sodome-ward they looke,
And as they toward the place their iourney tooke,
Said God, Shall I the thing from *Abram* hide
That I intend? he feares me, and beside,
He will instruct his children, keepe my hest,
And all earths nations shall in him be blest.
Then said the Lord, because that Sodomes crie
Is very great, and doth ascend the skie,
Yea and their sinne exceeding grieuous is,
I will go see how deeds agree with this.
Then *Abram* said, Lord shall the righteous fare
In punishment like those that wicked are?
Farre be it from the Iudge of all mens sight,
To do the thing that were not iust and right.
If fiftie good therein abode do make,
Wilt thou not spare it for those fifties sake?
If forty fiue, or thirtie, twentie, ten,
Wilt thou not spare it for those righteous men?
Yes, said the Lord, if onely ten there bee,
For all the rest thou shalt preuaile with me.
With that the Lord departed, mou'd to grace,
And *Abraham* return'd vnto his place.
Then in the euening (suns declining state)

As

As righteous *Lot* did sit at Sodome gate,
There came two Angels,which when he espide,
He did inuite them kindly to abide
Within his house that night,and wash their feete:
But they refusing,would remaine in streete:
Yet he importunate,they did consent,
And in with him those guests of heauen went,
Where he did entertaine them with a feast.
But ere the time was come they should take rest,
The Sodomites in multitudes were found,
Both old and yong the house enuiron'd round:
And calling *Lot*,said,Bring vnto our sight
Those men that harbor in thy house to night,
Let them come forth to vs,we may them know:
Then *Lot* intreates,My brethren do not so:
I haue two daughters,virgins both they be,
Which in affection are right deare to me,
Yet rather them Ile yeeld vnto your will,
Then these men should endure such hainous ill:
Oh let not sinne so wickedly incense,
Vnder my roofe they came for their defence.
With that they thrust the holy man aside,
And said,Stand backe,for this weele not abide,
Our furie shall the more towards thee appeere,
Art thou a Iudge that cam'st to soiourne here?
Wilt thou controule in that we go about?
Weele breake thy doore, our force shall fetch them out.

But preſſing forth,they could no entrance find,
For on a ſodaine all were ſtricken blind:
Blind bodies now,that had blind ſoules before,
Tiring themſelues in ſeeking out the dore.
Then ſaid the Angels vnto righteous *Lot*,
What friends haſt here (that we deſtroy them not)
Beſides thy daughters and thy ſonnes in law?
Out of the citie all thou haſt withdraw:
The crie is great before th'Almighties face,
And he hath ſent vs to deſtroy the place.
*Lot* did aduiſe his children,and the reſt,
But to his ſonnes in law it ſeem'd a ieſt:
They were ,as at this day moſt ſinners bee
Careleſſe,till vengeance they do feele and ſee.
When morning did darke nights blacke curtaines draw,
*(*Laſt morning that the Sodomites ere ſaw*)*
The Angels haſtned *Lot* to ſpeed away,
But as he did prolong the time with ſtay,
They caught him vp, his children, and his wife,
And brought him out,and bad him ſaue his life:
Looke not behind,nor in this plaine abide,
Leaſt thou do periſh: wherewith *Lot* replide,
My Lords,if fauour I haue found,take pitie,
And graunt me to enioy but yonder citie,
How ſhould I to the mountaines ſafely flie?
Some euill may betide,there I ſhall die,
Onely but *Soar* to thy ſeruant giue,

　　　　　　　　　　　　　　　　That

That litle *Soar*, and my foule fhall liue.
Thou haft preuaild (faid they) thy fute obtaine,
Go thither, and in fafetie remaine.
Now was the Sunne new rifen on earths face,
And *Lot* new entred in his refuge place,
When fodainly a fhewre from heauen fell,
Made Sodome feeme as Sodome had bene hell.
Twas no fuch element as wafht the ground,
When all the world (excepting eight) were **drownd:**
Then waters were the workers of Gods ire,
But now in vengeance he employes the fire,
An element of farre more fearfull kind,
Did finfull Sodome (turn'd to afhes) find.
No common fier, fit for needfull things,
But flames that dread, terror and anguifh **brings**
Of cruell torments, grieuous to be felt,
Of fulphur fauour lothfome to be fmelt,
Of terrible amazement to the eie,
A flaming citie, and a burning skie:
All was deftroyd of timber worke and **ftones,**
All was confum'd compofde of flefh and bones,
And Sodome which at euening did appeare,
As if a Paradife of God it were,
Seemd in the morning vnto *Abrams* eies,
As fmoake that from a fornace doth arife.

Ob-

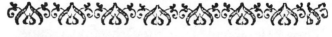

## Obdurate Pharaoh in his hard-
### nesse of heart.

MOses, what meſſage doeſt thou bring?
Am I not *Pharaoh*, Ægypts King?
I will not let the people go,
For all the wonders thou canſt ſhow.
Not *Arons* ſerpent-turning rod,
Shall make my heart obey your God.
My Sorcerers the like can doo:

*The tē plagues.*  Come Coniurers, make Serpents too.
1. The waters changing into blood,
   The fiſhes dying in the flood,
2. The frogs through all the land increaſt,
3. The lice offending man and beaſt:
4. Th'intolerable ſwarmes of flies,
5. The cattell that in Ægypt dies:
6. The ſwelling botches, ſores and blaines,
7. The thunder, haile and fire that raines:
8. Graſhoppers that all greene things waſt,
9. The darkneſſe that three dayes did laſt:
10. The ſtriking all the firſt-borne dead,
    To true conuerſion cannot lead.
    Hard is my heart and vnrelenting,

Tis

Tis vnacquainted with repenting:
*Moses*,euen by my kingly might,
I charge thee to depart my fight,
Vpon thy life fee me no more,
For if thou doeſt, thou di'ſt therefore.
My truſt doth in my ſtrength conſiſt,
Put confidence in whom thou liſt.
On horſe and chariot I depend:
Truſt in your God,let him defend.
Vnto the fea I will purſue
Thy Iſraelites,that ſlauiſh crue,
And there I will them all confound,
Or there let me and mine be drownd.

*The mirrour of Chaſtitie*.

FAire Hebrew, pleaſure of mine eyes,
To whom my loue I ſacrifice,
Thou haſt found fauour in her ſight,
Whoſe loue doth thy loue kind inuite,
To what delights I can afford,
To *Putiphar* great *Pharoes* Lord,
Before all loues in Ægypt bee,
Thy Ladie makes her choiſe of thee,
Why then inioy,and full poſſeſſe,

Vnto

Vnto my bed haue free acceſſe,
Where all the welcomes loue can make,
Shall entertaine thee for my ſake.
Be not ſo baſhfull,and a man,
Thou ſhouldſt court better then I can,
Being ſo louely euery part,
Except thy tongue that wanteth art;
Yet ſhe that may,bids thee be bold,
If I ſay ſeaze, preſume, take hold.
Why doeſt thou on vaine credit ſtand,
Vrging what truſt is in thy hand?
In that thy Lord exceeding large,
Committeth all things to thy charge,
Excepting me,all things beſide
Do vnder truſt with thee abide:
What of all this? I offer more
Then will be ſold for Ægypts ſtore.
What's gold to him that food doth need?
The mettall cannot hunger feed:
What's meate to him wants appetite?
Sickneſſe doth loath,though health inuite:
But loue doth choiſeſt welcome bring,
To loweſt beggar,higheſt king.
How oft haue I emboldned thee
With that kind word,*Come lie with mee?*
Where is thy ſence and manly ſprite,
That ſhould be ready to requite?

Wilt

Wilt thou ſo harſhly go away?
My hearts deſire, mild *Ioſeph* ſtay:
Doeſt turne thy backe? wilt not conſent?
By *Pharaoes* life thou ſhalt repent.
Ile keepe this garment to thy ſhame,
Thy Lord I vowe ſhall ſee the ſame.
Ile tell him, if I had not cride
I had bin forced to abide
Foule rauiſhment, which to preuent
Clamors vnto the skies I ſent,
And thou for feare that durſt not ſtay,
Leauing thy mantle, ranſt away.
This plot the harlot put in vre:
*Ioſeph* this ſlaunder did endure,
Yet ſtill continude conſtant chaſt,
With luſt allur'd, with lies diſgrac'd.

## Sampſon betrayed by Dalilah.

Onder of men, thou great in migh[t],
My hearts chiefe ioy, my ſoules delight,
Thou onely admirable man
Of all the ſtocke and tribe of *Dan.*
Thou that at *Thamnah* valiant did
Euen rend a Lion like a Kid.

D                         At

At Askalon in valour tride,
Where thirtie by thine owne hand dide:
That Azah gates with powrefull will,
Didſt carry vp to Hebron hill:
Oh let me craue a boone of thee,
As thou in loue ſhall gaine of mee.
Thy ſtrength to other men denide,
Great *Samſon* where doth that abide?
Oh proue thy ſelfe to me ſo kind,
As tell me but how I may thee bind:
Delude me not, kind ſweete, with mockes,
Not withes, nor tying of thy lockes
Is ought auailing thereunto:
Deere *Samſon*, tell me what to do.
Thrice by thee I haue bin deluded,
Now tell me where's thy might included?
Wilt thou this ſmall requeſt denay?
Wilt thou refuſe thy *Dalila?*
Then I reſolue thou lou'ſt me not,
For out of loue is all things got.
Thy ſute (quoth he) my deare, hath ſped,
There nere came razor on my head:
I haue bene from my mothers wombe
A Nazarite by heauens doome:
Loue, if my head be ſhauen bare,
I ſhall be weake as others are.
Then on her lap his head ſhe layd,

And

And with his curious lockes fhe playd,
And fo in dalliance did him keepe,
Till fhe had wantond him afleepe:
Then fent for one that fhau'd him quite
Of all the haire contain'd his might.
Which done, her fexes nature fhowes,
Betraid him inftant to his foes
The Philiftines, who him defpife,
And cruelly put out his eyes,
Then fet him in a mill to grind,
This woman-truft did *Samfon* find.

## King Sauls defpairefull Tragedie.

DAunted with feare of the Philiftines force,
Difanimated *Saul*, where fhall I flie?
  Of my diftreffe there's no man hath remorce,
To anfwer me by dreames God doth denie,
  No helpe by Prophets, all my comfort's fled,
  Oh *Samuel*, that man of God is dead.

I know inchantment is a grieuous fin,
And Ifraels God forbids it in his law,
Yet with a witch at Endor I haue bin,
To fpeake with *Samuel*, whofe fhape I faw

Appeare

Appeare in's mantle,reuerent,graue and old,
Who my deftruction and my end foretold.

Wherefore haft thou difturbed me he faid,
In caufing of me to be raifed thus?
I anfwered him,for that I was afraid
Of Philiftines,that vexe and trouble vs:
    And God is gone,he anfwers not at all,
    Oh tell what will become of wretched *Saul*.

Becaufe (quoth he) thou didft not God obay,
To execute on the Amalekites:
Therefore he hath done this to thee this day,
Thy difobedience thus his wrath requites,
    Thy kindome from thee he away hath rent,
    And giuen it *Dauid*, this is Gods intent.

Moreouer Ifrael and alfo thee,
The Lord will put in the Philiftins hands,
And euen to morrow fhalt thou be with mee,
Thou and thy fonnes,thus (*Saul*) thy kingdome ftands,
    Thy hoaft fubdude,thy felfe of life bereft,
    And thou become the man whom God hath left.

With this I fell defpairefull on my face,
My ftrength was gone with fafting and with feare:
O wretched man,depriued of Gods grace,

                        That

That mine owne end with dread did trembling heare,
To morow he hath tould me is the day
That Philiſtines my ſonnes and me will ſlay.

Come fatall day, come curſed Philiſtines,
The men of Iſrael now are forc'd to flie,
My three deare ſonnes their lateſt breath reſignes,
Mount Gilboa in thee their bodies lie,
    *Abinadab, Melchiſua, Ionathan,*
    Ile follow you with all the ſpeed I can.

See harneſſe-bearer, th'archers haue me found,
I will not haue them triumph in my death,
Oh draw thy ſword, I do intreate a wound,
Shew me the kindneſſe to depriue my breath:
    Art thou afraid to ſhed thy Princes blood?
    Why then my ſelfe will do my ſelfe that good.

This mine owne ſword the inſtrument Ile make
Of this my laſt and bloudy ſacrifice:
Vpon this point the worlds farewell Ile take:
Here the diſtreſſed King of Iſrael dies:
    He dies, that leaſt his foes ſhould glorying ſtand,
    Will kill himſelfe euen ready to their hand.

                                The

# The Virgine-sacrifice of Duke *Jepthahs daughter*.

THe mightie Marshall of the Israelites,
In armes against contending Amonites,
Soliciting th'Almightie for successe,
And whole depending on his powrefulnesse,
When he towards *Gilead* in armes did passe,
And thence to *Mispah* where proud *Ammon* was,
Vow'd if the victory he might obtaine,
Gainst those that held Gods people in disdaine,
And home returne a conqueror in peace,
His feruour to the Lord should so increase
In gratitude, that in most humble wise,
He to his Maiestie would sacrifice
What ere it were that his sight first beheld
Come forth his doore at his returne from field.
*Iephthah* in conquest to his hearts desire,
From *Aroer* a victor doth retire.
But here behold the end of *Amons* slaughter,
Begins the tragedie of his owne daughter:
To welcome him, all her endeuours striues,
True loue's most ioyfull when beloued thriues,
With daunces and with timbrels she doth meete him,
And all the solace she can make to greete him.

When

When he beheld his deare and onely child,
Surpriz'd with griefe, in raging humor wild,
He rent his clothes, and vnto heauens cride,
Oh worse then death the sight I now abide,
Thy presence all my fortunes doth confound,
Within a sea of teares mine eyes be drownd:
Most louing child, to God my vow is made,
With sacrifice of thee it must be paide.
Wherewith obediently she did reply,
Grieue not so much deare father that tis I:
To *Iacobs* God be faithfull in your vow,
Onely kind father, vnto me allow
Two months of mourning, to bewaile the state
Of my virginitie disconsolate:
Euen at the mountaines will I go and mourne,
And at the time appointed, thence returne.
His leaue she had, with mournfull maides attending,
Each one her griefe, and teares, and sorrow lending:
Their virgin teares compassions rules did keepe,
They waild for her, she mourn'd to see them weepe.
The time expir'd of her short stinted houres,
To him that had the guide of Israels powres,
She meekly came, and with most willing mind
For virgin-sacrifice her selfe resign'd.


                              Dauids

# Dauids combat with the Giant *of Gath*.

YOu men of Ifrael, feruants vnto *Saul*,
 *Goliah* founds defiance to you all:
 Your Soueraigne and his hoaft I do defie,
Bafe Ifraelites, a Philiftine am I.
Behold my ftature, tis fixe cubits long,
My helmet braffe, my coate of ftuffe as ftrong,
All likewife braffe, fiue thoufand fickles wayde:
My bootes are braffe, of braffe my fhield is made,
My fpeares fhaft, looke vpon it, and confeffe,
A Weauers beame in bignes, tis no leffe,
The very head thereof iron and fteele,
Sixe hundred weight, as fome of you fhall fcele.
Bring forth your champion, fingle me a man,
And Ile confeffe there's valour in you than.
Giue me a man I fay, and let vs fight,
Amongft you all find one ftout Ifraelite.
When *Dauid* heard this mightie man of Gath,
With terror breathing out his irefull wrath,
He did intreate a fauour of the King,
To combat that huge giant with a fling:

No

No other weapon but a ſtaffe he tooke,
And fiue ſmooth ſtones of choiſe out of the brooke:
So forth with courage reſolute he went:
The Philiſtine perceiuing his intent
To combat him, in ſtature but a child,
Diſdainfully in ſcoffing maner ſmild,
And ſaid to *Dauid*, What ſeeme I to be?
Belike a dog, thou bringſt a ſtaffe for me.
Now in the name of all the gods I ſerue,
I curſe thee, and as thou doeſt well deſerue
Thy fleſh for meate, the birds ſhall preſent ſhare,
Ile with thy gobbets feed the fowles of th'aire:
Thy carcaſſe on the ſodaine I will yeeld
For beaſts to prey vpon that are in field.
Thus did the Giant of his valour brag,
While *Dauid* tooke out of his ſhepheards bag
A ſtone, and ſlang the ſame into his head,
That he vnto the ground fell groueling dead.
Who when the Philiſtines beheld to fall,
Diſmaid in fearfull maner, they fled all,
And then that hand which the Almightie guided,
With his owne ſword his head from's trunke deuided:
Thus did the ſimple, weake, vpright and iuſt,
Subdue the ſtrong that in his ſtrength did truſt.

E    The

## The true Map of a dogged Miſer.

FRom *Pharan* wilderneſſe King *Dauid* ſent
Ten of his yong men, that to *Carmel* went
With kind ſalute, to an vnkind churle there,
*Nabal*, who at that place his ſheepe did ſheare.
Their Soueraignes meſſage to the wretch they tell,
And how his Maieſtie did greete him well,
No curious cates they came for to demand,
But what he pleaſde to giue came next to hand.
*Nabal* on them a frowning looke beſtowes,
And thus with tongue his dogged nature ſhowes:
What's *Dauid*, that I ſhould my victuals take,
And giue it run-awayes for *Dauids* ſake?
With *Iſays* ſonne, pray what haue I to do,
Haue I no vſe to put my meate vnto?
You may be vacabonds for ought I know,
Vpon ſuch fellowes nothing Ile beſtow,
Feed ſuch as you? yes marry twere good reaſon,
I haue mouths of mine owne to ſtop this ſeaſon:
Worke and be hang'd, earne it like other men,
Is't prouender you lacke? pray labour then:
Shall I take of my bread, my fleſh and drinke,
And giue to eu'ry raſcall, do you thinke?
No *Dauids* men, your maſter muſt prouide,

**Such**

Such hungry sharkes I neuer could adide:
Want he that will,my shearers shall not lacke,
Emptie you came,and so I pray go backe:
To him that sent you,tell him what I say,
My food must be emploid another way.
This churlish answer did so much incense,
*Dauid* vowde death should guerdon the offence:
Which when the wife of *Nabal* vnderstood,
She prudently preuented shedding blood,
And with a present,speedily did meete him,
Falling to ground euen at his feete to greete him:
Let not my Lord (said she) regard the man,
At whose offence thy wrath so late began,
Euen with his name his nature doth accord,
Folly is with him; but,my gracious Lord,
Thy hand-maid was not guiltie of the crime,
Nor did I see thy seruants at that time:
Successe attend thee wheresoere thou go,
Perish all they intend thy ouerthrow:
Accept the present,which my humble thought
In meekest dutie to my Prince hath brought.
Wherewith the kingly Prophet did replie,
Thou hast preuailed,*Nabal* shall not die,
I do reuerse my doome: a gracious wife
Hath sau'd a churlish,foolish,husbands life.

## The dead sleepe of Sisara.

REuengefull *Iabin*, King of Canaan,
Whose anceters great *Iosuah* had slaine,
To vexe the Israelites with warres began
At such time as in *Hazor* he did raigne,
His hoast by *Sisara* conducted was,
Who did vnto the riuer *Kison* passe.

Nine hundred chariots vnder his command,
When with ten thousand men neere *Thabor* hill,
*Barac* subduing them, had vpper hand,
And with the edge of sword his foes did kill:
*Sisara* in distresse constraind to light,
Was forc'd vpon his legs to take his flight.

And as he fled, most fearfull of his life,
Disanimated full of cares increase,
He came vnto the tent of *Habers* wife,
(For *Habers* house with *Iabin* was at peace)
*Iael* went forth and met him on the way,
And did intreate him to turne in and stay.

Turne in, my Lord, quoth she, be not afraid,
Repose thy weary limmes in *Iaels* tent,

For

For thou art welcome to thy poore hand-maid:
Then for a mantle prefently fhe went
　　To couer him,and fuch demeanor fhowes,
　　That moft fecure he did himfelfe fuppofe.

Oh I am tyr'd,faid he,and ouercome
In wearineffe,and cares orewhelmed deepe,
I thirft for water,pray thee giue me fome,
And then be centinell while I do fleepe,
　　Stand at the doore,and haue a fpeciall care
　　That none do intercept me vnaware.

If any chance to come enquire of thee
Who thou haft here,or what gueft is within,
Anfwer him then that no man thou didft fee,
For at thy tent there hath no creature bin:
　　Per forme this carefully at my requeft,
　　And fo he very foundly fell to reft.

The fleepe of death he flept on *Iaels* bed,
For fhe a hammer and a naile did take,
And driue it through the temples of his head,
That neuer after he had power to wake:
　　Thus he that from his foes his life did hide,
　　By his fuppofed friend a woman,dide.

## The Tragedie of Prince Absolom.

Mbition, I embrace thee in mine armes,
Scepter and Crowne are golden kingly charmes,
And haue preuail'd in my heroike minde,
Vnto a kingdomes rule, my heart's inclinde,
To be as high as Maiestie can sit,
Is the faire marke my thoughts desire to hit:
Why then ascend to *Dauids* royall throne,
Prince *Absolom* as King will sit thereon,
To fit my head euen with my fathers crowne,
Keeps filiall loue and subiect dutie downe:
In Hebron let the trumpets sound proclaime me,
And King of Israel let the Heralds name me:
My eares allow to heare no other sound,
But *Dauid* is deposde, his sonne is crownd:
Euen in the citie gates Ile causes heare,
And steale the hearts of all the people there.
Vpon the curteous that obeysance show,
A mild and sweete behauiour Ile bestow,
Kindnesse by art I will accomplish rare,
And how to please, shall be mine onely care:
Ile bow, Ile smile, Ile kindly giue embrace,
And shew a cheerfull looke, a louing face.
With *Dauids* gouernment, dislike Ile find,

Faining

Faining much griefe and paffion of the mind,
For euery wronged and oppreffed wight,
And wifh that I had powre their caufe to right:
From *Gilo* for *Ahitophel* Ile fend,
And worke that Counfellor to be my friend.
With euery fort making my faction ftrong,
Which done,Ile do no right,nor take no wrong.
My father growes already in difgrace,
And *Semei* hath curfde him to his face,
Threw ftones at him,and did him thus vpbraid,
*Come forth thou man of Belial*,he faid,
The Lord hath brought reuenge vpon thy head,
For all the blood that of *Sauls* houfe is fhed:
This doth difcourage him, animate me,
And tels my foule that I a King muft be.

    March on braue Ifralites,refolued powers,
Victorioufly preuaile,the day is ours,
Weel pitch our battell in this Ephraim wood,
Here let dead bodies glut the earth with blood,
Here *Dauids* crowne is either won or loft,
Here in this place it muft his kingdome coft,
Here of our liues we will be prodigall,
And that great monarch into queftion call:
Draw forth your fwords,let courage be their guide,
The controuerfie of a crowne decide,
Either a King,and all my foes conuince,
Or let me not remaine one hower Prince.

                       **Oh**

Oh cruell battell, fatall bloody day,
Vnto my death some mortall wound make way.
We are subdude, euen twentie thousand slaine,
Our scattred bodies on the earth remaine.
What shall I do? or whither shall I flie?
It is no matter, any where to die.
For shelter into this huge wood Ile ride,
Come on Despaire, be thou misfortunes guide.
Day turne to darknesse, and entinguish light,
And wrap my treason vp in vapory night.
Let not a little bird presume to sing:
Wither you trees, and leaues, and each greene thing.
Post on poore Mule, and spare no speed to run,
Thy riders race of life is almost done.
My royall birth is now of no esteeme,
My rarest beautie will deformed seeme:
Vengeance is come, Gods iudgement lights on mee,
I am caught hold off by a sensesse tree.
For my ambition, thus I mount on hie:
For pride, my lockes are ropes to hang me by.
Yonder comes *Ioab*, now my end is neare,
He brings my death vpon his bloody speare:
Come pierce me, captaine, rid this life from hence,
Fearefull my end, and grieuous my offence.
*Dauids* deare issue *Absolom* the faire,
Hangs without mercie bleeding in the aire.

Ahi-

## Ahitophels wiſedome conuer-
### ted to follie.

HOw is diſgrace impoſde vpon my head,
That for my counſell haue bene honored?
All Iſrael haue ſaid *Ahitophel*
Speakes euen as doth the heau'nly oracle:
Twas my aduiſe, none plotted it but I,
The Prince with's fathers concubines ſhould lie,
And he embrac'd it, and it ſorted well,
For as our expectation was, it fell.
And ſhall I chiefeſt ſtates-man in the land,
That ſtill in high affaires haue had a hand,
Be croſt by *Huſai* the Arachite?
No, firſt vpon my ſelfe ſhall vengeance light,
I ſaid twas beſt choſe out twelue thouſand men,
And ſet on *Dauid*, weary tired then
That inſtant night, being ouerworne and weake,
The hearts of all his people this would breake:
Vpon my life it was the onely way,
Yet *Huſai* hath croſt it with his nay:
He ſayes that *Dauid* and his men be ſtrong,
Th'are valiant, and haue had experience long.

F                    And

And like a Beare rob'd of her whelpes they be:
All this the Prince approues, reiecting me,
Thus of my wonted honor I haue mist.
But from this day, giue counsell he that list,
Ile home and take an order for my pelfe,
And then giue counsell how to hang my selfe,
My house shall be in order ere I die,
Then for my life, another course haue I:
Though out of order to the world it seeme,
Despaire and I thereof do well esteeme:
Not on my weapons point I meane to fall,
As did the desperate King, resolued *Saul*:
But to some fatall tree, I will repaire,
And hang my breathlesse bodie in the ayre.
Life, I detest thee, thou art almost done,
Time hold thy hand, with me the glasse is run:
Honor farewell, and in dishonor now,
I will go hang thee vp vpon some bough.
It was vaine honor did my heart intice,
And now ile sell it for a halters price:
All I haue learn'd in earthly honors schoole,
Is, worldly wise man proues a heauenly foole.

Salo-

## Salomons cenſure, in the two
### *Harlots controuerſie.*

TWo harlots ſtriuing with each other,
Would both vnto one child be mother,
And did to Wiſdomes King complaine,
That he true iuſtice would maintaine:
My Lord (ſaid one) iuſtice I craue,
Sayes tother, iuſtice let me haue:
We both within a houſe do lie,
She had a child, and ſo haue I,
Betweene their births but three dayes ſpace:
(Pray heare me I beſeech your grace)
Her child (my Soueraigne) in the night,
Of life ſhe hath depriued quite,
She ſmoothred it as I ſuppoſe,
And about midnight then ſhe roſe,
I being faſt aſleepe (God wot)
My liuing child away ſhe got,
And thruſt her dead one vnto me,
(This is as true, as true may be)
When in the morning I did wake,
Intending mine owne child to take:
And giue it ſucke, I found it dead,
Which when I did behold with dread,

F 2                         Viewing

Viewing it well with weeping eyne,
I plainely ſaw twas none of mine.
The tother harlot did reply,
An't pleaſe your Grace, this is a lie,
I neuer changed child for child,
Neither will I be thus beguild,
To take hers dead for mine aliue:
Would God that I might neuer thriue,
If that the liuing be not mine.
Thou lieſt (ſaid tother) tis not thine,
Thou ſhalt not, dame, delude me ſo,
My louing babe I well do know,
The very cheekes, the eyes, the noſe,
The mothers fauour plainly ſhowes,
Thy ſelfe (I will be ſworne) did ſay,
Twas wondrous like me tother day,
And now forſooth it is your owne,
How ſhameleſſe (Lord) this world is growne?
My gracious Prince (ſayes tother) heare,
Vpon my ſoule (great King) I ſweare,
If with this child ſhe haue to do,
Then ſhe is mother of them two:
The dead child is her owne in troth,
Now this ſhe claimes, ſo ſheele haue both.
I do deny the dead ſaid ſhe,
The liuing child belongs to me:
Oh God, art thou ſo voide of ſhame,

*Another*

Another womans fruite to claime?
Wilt thou ſtand ſtout in that's vntrue,
And ſay my infant is thy due?
When in thy conſcience thou art ſure
The paines for it I did endure,
The mothers griefe when it was borne:
Fie wicked woman, I would ſcorne
To beare ſo bad and leud a mind,
I grieue thou art of woman kind.
Then ſaid the King, this ſtrife Ile end,
You both for one liue child contend,
That child Ile with a ſword deuide,
And giue to each of you a ſide,
A iuſt diuiſion I will make,
And halfe a child ſhall either take.
Then ſpake the mother whoſe it was,
Dread Lord let no ſuch ſentence paſſe,
But rather with my heart I craue,
The liue child wholy let her haue.
Nay, but ſayes tother to the King,
As thou haſt ſpoke performe the thing,
Nor mine, nor thine let it remaine,
But ſhare it equall twixt vs twaine.
Then ſaid the King, the babe ſhall liue,
And to the mother I it giue,
Which I am ſure thou canſt not bee,
Becauſe no kindneſſe reſts in thee.

F 3                                    Cruell

## Cruell Queene Iezabel turned
### *vnto dogges meate.*

WHat terror is my spirit vexed in ?     (eares?
How doth Reuenge sound dolefull to mine
My soule's pursude with that same crying sin
Of murther, *Naboth* fils my thoughts with feares.
     There is no horror like a troubled mind,
     As I accursed *Iezabel* do find.


Reuenge for bloud, I heare continuall sound,
Till vengeance comes, thus will it euer crie,
My soule is lost to get a little ground,
I caus'd the guiltlesse man, causlesse to die:
     I wrote a letter in my husbands name,
     And onely I the wicked plot did frame.


By my aduice a fast there was pretended,
And *Naboth* plac'd, amongst the chiefest then
Being suddenly accus'd to haue offended
By two suborned, leud and diuellish men,
     Who to the Elders did auouch this thing:
     The Iezralite blasphem'd God and the king.

                                           Vpon

Vpon this ſlandrous falſe accuſing breath,
He ſentenc'd was to die with common voice,
And preſently they ſtoned him to death,
Which I no ſooner heard, but did reioyce,
    And went to *Ahab*, ſaying, Ioyfull be,
    The vineyard now is thine, ile giue it thee.

Going to take poſſeſſion of the ſame,
He meeteth with *Elias* by the way,
Sent from the Lord, who tels him in his name:
Hearke bloudie purchaſer what God doth ſay:
    Haſt thou both kil'd and got poſſeſſion too?
    For this thy ſin, marke what the Lord will doo.

Euen in the place where dogs did licke the bloud
Of *Naboth*, to whoſe vineyard thou mak'ſt claime:
Euen in that place, the Lord hath thought it good,
That dogs ſhall with thy bloud performe the ſame:
    Euill on thee and on thy ſeed ſhall fall,
    From thee, to him makes water gainſt the wall.

And for thy wife, thus ſaith the God of power,
Since ſhe hath wrought ſuch euill in his eyes:
Dogges ſhall the fleſh of *Iezabel* deuoure,
When by the citie wals her carcaſe lies:
    In Iezrael it ſhall be ſhortly ſeene,
    That dogs ſhall eate thy proud and painted Queene.
                                    Which

Which punifhment reuenging *Iehu* wrough*,
In rooting out the houfe of *Ahab* quite,
*Ioram* he flue,and caufed to be brought
Vnto the plot of ground was *Naboths* right,
    Then to the citie did in triumph ride,
    Where me moft wretched murdreffe hee fpide.

My face was painted,euen as pride would haue it,
My head attyr'd to vanities content,
Thus at a window I did ftand to braue it,
Said *Iehu*,who is there to my fide bent?
    With that were chamberlaines at hand lookt out,
    The inftruments to bring my death about.

He bad them throw me downe,and fo they did,
They fent me with a vengeance to the ground,
My blood dafht out,my life was fodaine rid,
Deuouring dogs my flefh had quickly found.
    And with a Queene they fild their paunches full,
    Leauing but palmes of hands,my feete and fcull.

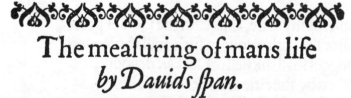

# The meafuring of mans life
## *by Dauids fpan.*

THreefcore and ten,the age and life of man,
In holy *Dauids* eyes feem'd but a fpan:

                          For

For halfe that time is loſt and ſpent in ſleepe,
So onely thirtyfiue for vſe we keepe.
Then dayes of youth muſt be abated all,
Wiſe *Salomon*, childhood and youth doth call
But vanitie, meere vanitie he ſayes,
All that doth paſſe vs in our infant dayes:
Our time of age we take no pleaſure in,
Our dayes of griefe we wiſh had neuer bin,
Then ſleepe deducted, youth, and age, and ſorrow,
Onely a ſpan is all thy life doth borrow.

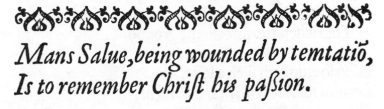

*Mans Salue, being wounded by temtatiõ,*
*Is to remember Chriſt his paſſion.*

THe wounds that Ieſus ſuffred for my ſin,
  Are mouthes that cry, Oh loue him with thy heart:
The thornes that pierced through his ſacred skin,
Are tongues, pronouncing Loue is his deſert:
The tort'ring whips that did to anguiſh moue him,
Are echoes, ſounding, Wretched ſinner loue him.

*There is no loſſe, that griefe can get againe,*
*But loſſe of grace, ſorrow may grace attaine.*

G          Salomons

## Salomons good houſwife, in the
### 31. *of his Prouerbs*.

HE that a gracious wife doth find,
Whoſe life puts vertue chiefe in vre,
One of the right good houſwife kind,
That man may well himſelfe aſſure,
And boaſting ſay that he hath found
The richeſt treaſure on the ground.

Who ſo enioyeth ſuch a loue,
Let him reſolue with hearts conſent,
She euer conſtantly will proue
A carefull nurſe, want to preuent,
With diligence and painfull heed,
Preuenting taſt of beggars need.

And while ſhe liues will ſtill procure,
By true and faithfull induſtrie,
T'increaſe his wealth, and to inſure
His ſtate in all ſecuritie:
To ſeeke his quiet, worke his eaſe,
And for a world no way diſpleaſe.

Her

Her houſhold folke from ſloth to keepe,
She will endeuour with good heed,
At worke more wakefull then aſleepe,
With flaxe and ſtuffe, which houſwiues need
   To be employd, her hands alſo
   The way to worke will others ſhow.

Her wit a common wealth containes,
Of needments for her houſhold ſtore,
And like a ſhip her ſelfe explaines,
That riches brings from forraine ſhore,
   Ariuing with a bounteous hand,
   Diſpearſing treaſure to the land.

Before the day ſhe will ariſe
To order things, and to prouide
What may her family ſuffice,
That they at labour may abide,
   If ſhe haue land, no paine ſhall want
   To purchaſe vines, ſet, ſow, and plant.

No honeſt labour ſheele omit,
In ought ſhe can attaine vnto,
But will endeuour ſtrength and wit,
Adding the vtmoſt ſhe can do:
   And if that profit comes about,
   By night her candle goes not out.

G a        A

A willing hand to the diſtreſt
She lends, and is a chearefull giuer:
Come winters cold and froſtie gueſt,
When idle huſwiues quake and quiuer,
 She and her houſhold's cloathed well,
 The weathers hardneſſe to expell.

Her skill doth worke faire tapiſtrie,
With linnen furniſh'd of the beſt:
Her needle workes do beautifie,
And ſhe in ſcarlet coſtly dreſt,
 When Senators aſſembled be,
 Her husbands honor there ſhall ſee.

Her ſpinning ſhall her ſtore increaſe,
The fineſt cloth ſhall yeeld her gaine,
And daily profit ſhall not ceaſe,
Which her vnidle hands maintaine:
 Her clothing ſhall her worth expreſſe,
 And Honors yeares her end poſſeſſe.

Her mouth ſhall neuer opened be,
But wiſedome will proceede from it :
And ſuch mild gracious words yeelds ſhee,
Sweetneſſe vpon her tongue doth ſit:
 In age ſhe will her care addreſſe,
 To eate no bread of idleneſſe.

         **Her**

Her children shall their dutie show ,
Most reuerent to her all their life,
Her husband blesse, that he did know
The time to meete with such a wife:
    And vttring foorth his happinesse,
    Her vertues in this wise expresse.

I know t'is true that more then one
Good huswife there is to be found :
But I may say, that thou alone
Aboue all women dost abound,
    Yea I protest in all my dayes,
    Thou art the first, and thee ile praise.

What thing is fauour but a shade ?
It hath no certaine lasting hower,
Whereof is wanton beautie made,
That withers like a Sommers flower?
    When these shall end their date in dayes,
    She that feares God shall liue with praise.

And such a wife of worthie worth,
Due glories lot will to her fall,
And great assemblies will giue forth
What vertues shee's adorn'd withall,
    Her lifes renowne to fame shall reach,
    Her good example others teach.

# Salomons Harlot, in the 2.7.and 8. *chapt. of his Prouerbs.*

A Harlot of the whorifh kind
Defcrib'd by Wifedomes King,
  Whofe paths are crooked and whofe wayes
Vnto deftruction bring:

That impudent with fhamelefse brow,
Doth modeft life deteft,
And of all brutifh filthynefse
Infatiate is pofsft,

Is noted to be full of words,
And doth the ftreets frequent,
Not qualited as *Sara* was,
To keepe within the tent.

But haunts the citie to be feene
Of all that pafseth by,
Cal's fimple people voyd of fence,
Her kindnefse to come try.

Like curl'd and painted *Iefabel,*
She at her doore will fit,

To

To draw men from their ftraighteft wayes,
To come and enter it.

My bed (quoth fhe) is finely deckt,
And garnifht curioufly,
With cloth of Ægypt, Aloes, Myrre,
And coftly tapiftry.

Come let vs take our fill of loue,
Be thou my gueft to night,
Till morning let vs pleafe our felues
In taking lufts delight.

The waters that are got by ftealth,
Are with much fweetneffe grac'd:
The bread that's eaten priuily,
Doth yeeld a pleafant taft.

My husband is not to be fear'd,
Of this thy felfe perfwade,
I know his iourney is of ftay,
By his prouifion made.

Thus with her falfe enticing tongue,
She doth allure to fin,
The foolifh graceleffe creatures heart,
That wants chaft thoughts within.

Care-

Careleſſe into the ſlaughter houſe
He enters with the oxe,
And like an ideot merily
Goes laughing to the ſtockes.

O keepe thy feete from wandring there,
For who ſo treads her path,
Is entred in deſtructions way
Of horror, vengeance, wrath.

The ſtrongeſt men haue bin deſtroyd
With her alluring breath,
Her houſe is euen the way to hell,
Her chamber harbors death.

All thoſe that vnto her do go,
Retire not backe againe
To take hold of the way of life,
But out of grace remaine.

Deſtruction doth enuiron round
The place of her abode,
And all her courſe of wicked life,
Is oppoſite to God.


A

# A description of heauenly Ferusalem.

CElestiall citie, built by wondrous art,
Most costly rich, most curious rarely wrought,
Where heau'nly skill doth plenteously impart
More then can euer enter humane thought,
Fram'd by the power of that great Architect,
Which by his word that wonder did erect.

The situation is aboue the skies,
Of this most sanctified holy place,
Tis onely seene by Saints and Angels eyes,
Those citizens by Gods eternall grace,
For all eternitie are resident
In that for-euerlasting monument.

The longitude and latitude is one,
Foure square, the wall doth high and large appeare,
In shine like to a precious Iasper stone,
As Cristall in transparent brightnesse cleare:
Twelue gates, that frō twelue tribes deriue the name,
And euery gate an Angell at the same.

H                    Three

Three on the Eaſt ſide, three vpon the Weſt,
Three on the South, and three vpon the North,
Made of twelue pearles, the rareſt, orient, beſt,
For heauen hath in perfection things of worth:
    The pureſt gold is pauement for the ſtreete,
    Which ſhines like glaſſe vnder their glorious feete.

The wals foundation precious doth conſiſt,
Of Iaſper, Saphir, and the Calcedon,
Of Topaze, Iacinth, and the Amethiſt,
Beryll and Chriſolite tis founded on,
    Sardius, Chryſopraſus, Emeraud,
    Theſe the celeſtiall Arteiſt do applaud.

Of no Sunne light this citie ſtands in need,
Nor any ſhining that the Moone can lend,
For from Gods preſence and the Lambe proceed
A brightneſſe that ſo glorious doth extend.
    Thoſe diuine dwellers haue eternall light,
    An euerlaſting day that knowes no night.

There ſhall be heard no mournfull ſound of cries,
No kind of ſorrow cauſing to complaine,
But God will wipe away all teares from eyes,
And free them euer from the ſenſe of paine:
    He that doth promiſe this, is faithfull, true,
    *The old is paſt, and all things ſhall be new.*

                                        **The**

The Kings of th'earth ſhall bring their glory there,
To treaſure it in glories habitation:
And all the holy men that euer were,
Shall there enioy their heauenly expectation:
   *Abel* the iuſt, *Noah* in righteouſneſſe,
   And perfect *Abraham* with his faithfulneſſe.

Obedient *Iſacke*, *Iacobs* bleſſed ſeed,
Meeke *Moſes* that great Prophet of the Lord,
The valiant *Ioſuah*, choſen and decreed
To fight Gods battels with a powrefull ſword,
   *Dauid* the man after Gods hearts deſire,
   Is their chiefe ſinger in the Angels quire.

And all Gods ſeruants in their foreheads ſealed,
A hundred foure and fortie thouſand Saints,
To whom this cities glory is reuealed,
Them with true life eternall he acquaints,
   Of *Rubens* tribe, *Gads*, *Iuda's*, *Simeons*,
   *Aſers*, *Manaſſes*, *Leuies*, *Zabulons*.

*Iſſachars*, *Beniamins*, and *Nephthalies*,
*Ioſephs* deſcent, of each twelue thouſand ſigned,
Theſe do behold that which by earthly eyes
Cannot beſeene, nor by mans tongue defined,
   The glory is ſo wondrous infinite,
   No heart, tong, hand, can thinke, can ſpeake, can write.

There doth the great and countlesse summe remaine,
Of euery nation, people, kindred, tong,
Whose multitude no number can explane,
Before the throne in vestures white and long:
    These haue the palmes of victory beside,
    And do in presence of the Lambe abide.

There is no danger of inuading fo,
That of those ioyes the blessed can depriue:
No bloudy enemy may thither go,
The lurking Viper cannot there ariue,
    No deadly sighted Basiliske to feare,
    The auncient Serpents hissing none shall heare.

But the soft breathing of the holy Ghost,
Wherein Gods glory shall reuealed be,
Perfections fulnesse, and the chiefest most,
That Saints and Angels can desire to see,
    Shall in abundant maner be exprest,
    Vnto those happie euerliuing blest.

In this secure and peacefull habitation,
Shall no vncleane thing come or haue accesse;
For whosoeuer workes abhomination,
Must be excluded from that happinesse:
    Those that are there with glory to be crownd,
    Their names must in the booke of life be found.

Without

Without are dogs,whoremungers,murderers,
And whofoeuer loues or maketh lies,
Graceleſſe inchanters,and idolaters,
For entrance vnto theſe the Lambe denies,
    They are for horror and eternall wo,
    And muſt with trembling to deſtruction go.

O ſonnes of *Adam*,ſinfull race of clay,
Moſt miſerable blind deceiued men,
You ſcattred ſheepe that wander from the way,
If this place be your fold,where ſtray you then?
    Why is your pace to heauen ſo ſlow and ſlacke?
    Or rather,why from thence retire you backe?

O fooliſh louer of vaine earthly things,
Why ſeek'ſt thou honor and promotion here?
Which onely care,griefe and vexation brings,
To build, to purchaſe, and let leaſes deare:
    Ioyne houſe to houſe,and pile vp gold beſide,
    Fixing thy thoughts on gaine,thy heart on pride.

Thou neuer canſt attaine like bleſſedneſſe,
In the inioying all thy ſoule can craue,
Nor once come neare taſt of the happineſſe,
That the leaſt ſeruant in Gods houſe ſhall haue:
    For in this holy citie where they liue,
    Is treaſure,which the world can neuer giue.

H 3                    Which

Which shall endure perpetually their lot,
The lot and portion in the liuing land,
A giuers gift, whose purpose alters not,
But for the length of endlesse time shall stand
    In all perfection and securitie,
    True holinesse and perfect puritie.

When thou with this worlds pompe and dignity,
Which here on earth did please thy soule so well,
Shalt beare that same rich glutton company,
Whose burial's in the dreadfull vault of hell,
    Excluded from all mercy, comfort, grace,
    In that same endlesse, easelesse, hopelesse place.

---

### *Times swiftnesse.*

I Run, I flie, I neuer stand at stay,
   There's no recalling of me being past,
Wise men take hold, and meet me in the way,
Fooles first neglect, their late repent comes last:
    He that will vse me to his endlesse gaines,
    Must spend time well while he on earth remaines.

### *Mans negligence.*

I Had a time in youth for learnings treasure,
  I had a time to haue attained grace,

I

I spent that time in worlds bewitching pleasure,
And wish for time now time hath turn'd his face.
 Time runs before, and instantly forsakes vs,
 Death posts behind, and sodaine ouertakes vs.


*Deaths powerfulnesse.*


I Make all feare, that am a fearlesse creature,
 The world doth euen tremble at my name,
Ender I am of all begun by nature,
Proud flesh and blood in graues of earth I tame:
 Though bitter vnto many, sweet to some
 That loath this life for loue of life to come.

# A view of this world  the Globe
## *of Vanitie.*

L Ooke, mortals, on this stage of earthly things,
 View well the changes of inconstant time,
 Begin at poore men, and go vp to kings,
From humble hearts, to such as loue to clime,
From innocents, to such as liue by crime,
 From low to high, from high againe to low,
 What man is he would worlds delights forgo?

Oh

## 64

Oh fond felicitie that all men find,
On this vnfetled pauement of the earth!
Where's nothing but perplexitie of mind,
None prouing ftill the period to our mirth,
Backe from our graue to our firft houre of birth:
    Onely this blindneffe doth fome fooles befot,
    They liue in forrow, and they fee it not.

For what's a King, or mightie potent Lord,
That like a god, millions of people fwayes?
That faues and kils with his commanding word,
Whofe will the flattrer fooths, and all obayes,
Pray what's the pleafure of his kingly dayes?
    If he be good (as great men good is rare)
    His kingdome then is but his hourely care.

What's a great conqueror, whofe name is fear'd,
Like *Cæfar*, or the dreaded *Tamberlaine?*
Who by his fword, Piramides hath rear'd,
With bones and fcalpes, and enfignes of the flaine,
Looke on him well and find him meerly vaine,
    The fitttteft Epithet for him is this,
    *This mightie man, a mightie murdrer is.*

What's a great traueller by fea and land,
That doth furuey the world with curious eye?
And fees what wonders the Creators hand

                        Wrought

Wrought in the deepes, in vales, or mountaines hie.
Who doth not thinke this traueller doth lie,
  Though he tell truth? then what's a greater shame
  For man to toile and get a liers name?

What is it to be rich and pile vp store,
To build great houses, titling them our owne,
To haue abundance, yet still couet more,
To rise by many wrong'd and ouerthrowne,
What is all this when it is truly knowne?
  *Misers oppresse, build, gather, to this end,*
  *For vnthrift heires to ruine, spoile and spend.*

What is it to be great in peoples eyes,
And to be puft vp with their bubble praise?
What is the issue of their vulgar cries,
Their songs and rimes, and high applauding layes?
Here's onely all, it shortens honors dayes:
  *Whom the rude greete with shouts and garlicke breath,*
  *The mightie hate, and hasten vnto death.*

What is it to be faire, and so composed,
That being earth, we yet seeme angeline?
To haue in vs all beauties grace inclosed,
And *Venus* fooles account vs most diuine?
What is the end to be thus goodly fine?
  On beauties brow is this inscription plac'd,
  *Tis rare to find a person faire and chast.*

I                                    What

What is it to be any thing indeed,
That mortals in their dull conceits commend?
What is it on the worlds delights to feed,
And haue each vanitie on vs attend?
Euen nothing all, for here's of all the end,
    As we were borne with teares to liue in paine,
    Death comes with fighes and takes vs hence againe.

---

## *A fumme of good defires.*

GReat God which haft al wifdome at commanding,
Be in my head, infpire my vnderftanding:
Almightie God, the obiect of true light,
Be thou director of mine eyes and fight:
Dread God, whofe word is facred and diuine,
Be in my mouth, and guide this tongue of mine:
Mercifull God, the fulneffe of all grace,
Be in my heart, and purge that filthy place:
Eternall God, on whom I whole depend,
Be at my laft departing and mine end.

---

## *Times Epigramme.*

STep *Cæfar* on earths ftage, and act thy part,
Shew now what monarch of the world thou art:
Let *Alexander* in his bones appeare,
That worlds commaunder while he liued here.

                        Come

Come *Nero* with a fheete about thine eares,
See who thy tyrannie regards or feares.
*Achilles* rowfe thy felfe from out thy toombe,
And fee what man will giue thy weapon roome.
*Hector*, with that renowmed *Hanniball*,
What are you now but rotten fellowes all?
You had a time of greatneffe, now tis fled,
And euen as fuch had neuer bin, y'are dead.
I knew you when with dread you made men bow,
Then dy'd, turn'd duft, and fo are nothing now.
Euen with the worlds creation I began,
And haue feene all the courfe of finfull man,
His ftate in Paradife that glorious place,
His difobedience, and his fall from grace,
His banifhment forth *Eden* for offending,
And fo from age to age, all times defcending,
Vntill this inftant yeare, fixe hundred fiue,
All that are dead, and euery one aliue
Is in my regifter, I note them well,
There's not a deed they do, but *Time* can tell.
Earth is a ftage, and mortals actors be,
That play before my fellow *Death* and me
All tragedies, for not a day you haue,
But fome are kild, and caried to their graue.
There goes the King from his imperiall feate,
Euen with the begger, for to be wormes meate:
There noble and ignoble, foole and wife,

I 2

Shall

Shall lie and rot till the firſt dead man riſe,
And there all that haue bin do certaine ſhow,
That all which are to come, muſt thither go.

## What one man likes, another lothes.

VNto himſelfe as each man hath his mind,
  Seuerall diſtinguiſht in his appetites,
So are his thoughts as variouſly inclind,
One liking theſe, another thoſe delights:
    Some greedy hindes account the greateſt pleaſure
    Onely conſiſteth in the gaining treaſure.

One loues no life, but where the trumpet ſterne,
Breaths deadly ſummons to oppreſſiue armes,
Caring not where, gainſt Spaniard or the Kerne,
So he may liue in martiall hot alarmes:
    He with *Tiphous* dares to giue aduenture,
    To raiſe a mount, the frame of heauen to enter.

One being wrapt with forraine admiration,
Of lawes, of cuſtomes, and of peoples natures,
Longing to know the climates variation,
Of monuments remote to ſee the ſtatures,
    How dangerous ſo ere delights to range,
    Till proofe approues the worſt in greateſt change.
                                                    Others

Others to chafe the timerous Hart delight,
Cheering the hounds with hornes rechanting blaft,
When fome applaud the towring Faulcons flight,
That now hath ceaz'd the moore-bred Mallard faft,
    And fome account as loft to be that day,
    When their eftates they hazard not at play.

But thou *Calliope* my Mufe diuine,
Mak'ft me neglect thefe fruitleffe vanities,
Thou doeft my fpirits from groffe earth refine,
Making my thoughts at future glory rife,
    For when the hinde, the fouldier, wandring knight,
    Starues, fals, clay clothes, fhall poefie giue light.

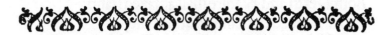

# The Araignement of the world
## *at Gods generall Seßions.*

WHen that great day of finners dolefull feare,
    The day of iudgement for the quicke & dead,
    Shall bring to doome all deeds that euer were,
With terror, trembling, horror, woe, and dread,
    The world fhall be reduc'd to afhes quite,
    And all flefh ftand amaz'd to fee that fight.

I 3                    What

What man by tongue or pen can make it knowne,
The horror that mens hearts ſhall then partake:
When the great Iudge of men ſits on his throne,
And euery one a iuſt account muſt make,
    In this diſtreſſed ſtate what's to be done:
    Which way ſhall ſinners flie, or whither runne:

The Prophets do giue witneſſe to this day,
And haue affirmed it will certaine come:
Our Sauiour warneth vs to watch and pray,
With preparation for that fearfull doome,
    When ſounding trumpe ſhall ſummon to appeare,
    And yeeld account what liues we liued here.

Both Death and Nature ſhall amazed ſtand,
To ſee reuiued humane creatures riſe,
The ſea ſhall yeeld her dead, as well as land,
All thoſe that in her watery boſome lies,
    Muſt make apparance at the Angels ſound,
    As well as they had graues vpon the ground.

Then ſhall each ſecret conſcience be reuealed,
The bookes of humane life be opened wide,
Not the leaſt thought can paſſe away concealed,
But all in publike knowledge ſhall abide,
    All hidden things obſcur'd within the hart,
    And each receiue his merit and deſart.

                             **What**

What can the sin-defiled creature say?
What aduocate will serue his case to pleade?
Since the vprightest man that liues this day,
Is debtor vnto hell and endlesse dread,
  Worthy of nothing for his best done deeds,
  If God in iustice gainst his sin proceeds.

O thou that freely doest of mercy saue,
Vprightest Iudge, whom bribes cannot seduce,
Pardon of thee on my soules knees I craue,
My guilt is great, and I haue no excuse.
  Remember Lord thou didst to earth repaire,
  Of sinfull man thou hadst such louing care.

Wilt thou permit (O Lord) thy grieuous paine,
Thy hunger, thirst, thy tortures, wounds and death,
Shall all be spent on my poore soule in vaine?
Yea that same willing yeelding vp thy breath
  To God thy Father, to procure my peace,
  Shall vtterly in power and vertue cease?

Suffer not Lord, the true effect to perish,
Of thy most bitter grieuous bloudy passion,
My fainting sprite thereby reuiue and cherish,
Thy bitter death's my sweet'st consolation:
  Mild Iesus, I most meekly do intreate,
  Shew mercy on me from thy iudgements seate.
                                        Guiltie

Guiltie I am, my guilt I do confeſſe,
Therefore I ſigh, and vnto thee retire,
Refuſe me not, thy mercies are not leſſe,
Then when the theefe obtained his deſire,
   And ſinfull *Magdalene* did fauour find,
   Thy pitie is the ſame, thou ſtill as kind.

For in a danger ſo extreme as this,
To whom for ſuccor might I ſafely flie,
To find aſſured comfort, and not miſſe?
But vnto thee thou ſupreme of the skie,
   Worthleſſe my prayers to come before thy face,
   Vnleſſe thy mercy ſit in iuſtice place.

Direct my feete that ſtray and wander wide,
And ſhadow me with thy protections wings,
Set me from goates, vpon the right hand ſide,
And place me where thy Saints and Angels ſings,
   To ſpeake thy praiſes with a heauenly voyce,
   Where ſoule and body endleſſe may reioyce.

## FINIS.

# HVMORS
## ANTIQVE
### *FACES.*

Drawne in proportion to his feuerall
Antique leftures.

*LONDON*
Imprinted for *Henry Rockett* , and are to bee
folde at the long Shop vnder S. Mildreds Church
in the Poultrie. 1605.

## To the Reader.

HE that to pleafe all humors doth intend,
May well begin but neuer make an ende :
S nec euerie humor hath his feuerall vaine,
Which in themfelues ftrange obiects doe retaine
I then will write at random : hit as t'will ,
If fome be pleaf'd fome be vnpleafed ftill.
To him that likes it beft, to him I fend it,
Miflike is not till you your felfe can mend it.
Then if my humor hath done humors wrong
Ile rather mend it or elfe hould my tongue.
Meane while comment but rightly on the text
I will prefent ftrange fafhions to you next.

A 2                              Vnder

## *Prologue.*

VNder the shadowe of the gloomy night,
 When silent sleepe arrests each mortall wight,
When fayrie *Oberon* and his night Queene
In *Cinthias* honor friskes ore euerie greene.
Sleepe, parting from mee, gaue inuention light
To finde some subiect for my pen to wright.
When musing how the world I best might fit,
I saw how Poets humor'd out their wit.
Nay then thought I write all of what they list,
Once in my daies ile proue a humorist.
When on the Sudden as I thought the thing,
I was encountred by the Fayrie King.
Mortall (quoth hee) I charge thee to ingage,
Thy pen to scourge the humors of this age,
Thou shalt not neede to make a long relation,
What thou canst get by tedïouse obseruation.
Fayrics haue left their lowe infernall places,
The seuerall formes of humors in their faces.
Take what, and where thou list while it is night,
But send them home before the day be light.

O by

## Epigram.

O By your leaue I pray you giue them vent,
Heere comes braue courtſhip gallant complement
Hee meetes his friend nay then he keepes a ſtur,
Illuſtrous, generous, moſt accompliſht Sur.
Kiſſes his hand and ſends it to his foote
As if he ought ſome ductie to his boote.
*Phœbus* bright lampe good halfe an houre might burne,
Courtly contending, each doth keepe his turne.
Vntill their Courtſhip peſter ſo the way,
By comes a cart, and then diſſolues the fray.
Then out comes wordes more eloquent then Hermes,
The quinteſſence of all your Inkehorne termes.
As we are Alians I am ſorrie thoe,
Tis your defect Sir: you will haue it ſoe.
Moſte admirable be the wordes they ſpeake,
T' expreſſe their mindes plaine engliſh is to weake.
To theſe ſtrange wordes, which theſe braue gallants
A courtly conge is the Epilogue.                    (cogge,
For hauing now ſo frankely ſpent their ſtore,
Needes muſt they parte when they can ſpeake no more

A 3                    A hand-

### Epigram.

A Hanfome fellow and a proper Squire,
A little hanging would promote him higher,
A man I tell you of the better forte,
Amongſt his equals hath a good reporte,
His dealings on the market day doth fall
At newgate market, Cheape and Leaden-Hall.
He is a taker, indeede is he foe,
I meane a taker vp of Purſes thoe:
This fellowe comming lately downe Cheape-fide,
A femall bootie ſuddenly eſpide.
Twas Market day, but quight out of his minde:
For he had left his Inſtruments behinde.
But his conceite that is no barren ſpring,
With little muſing had bethought a thing.
Was it the womans lucke or fortune whether
That ſhe ſhould weare both purſe and knife together?
The Cut-purſe ſwore and bound it with a curſe,
The womans knife ſhould cut the womans purſe,
And did it too   good reaſon by my troth,
For would you that a man ſhould breake his oathe,
Twas not for neede I pray conceaue the beſt,
His humor was to cut a Purſe in ieſt.

                                      Roome

### Epigram.

ROome Sirs, I pray for Bachus Cousen heere,
Whose paunch (the fatal tombe to al good cheare)
Welters in tallowe and huge cakes of grease,
Such burlie fellowes make good men of peace,
He is of such a huge insatiat size
His whole daies worke nothing but gurmandize.
He has a belly circular and rounde,
Is neuer full, O sir it is profound.
He has a huge and dreadefull fierie nose,
God blesse Paules steeple when hee puffes and blowes,
He dares not goe vngirded not two meales,
For then his guts would fall about his heeles.
Poore Painters were vndone if he were dead,
They loose the patterne of a Sarzens head,
I met him once riding downe Holborne late,
I surely thought the mouth at Bishops-gate
Had been on progresse, out in Oxfordshire
For to deuoure all Mutton and porredge there.
Well blame not him, he has a care to carue,
For otherwise poore church-yard wormes wold starue.
Sweete

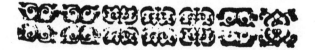

## Epigram.

Sweete Signeor ſwaſh was late orecome with paſsion
Becauſe his life was quite worne out of faſhion:
For he proteſts, nay and you wil, heele ſweare
That he hath bin in London halſe a yeare.
Yet all this while that hee in London lay:
Twas not his luckeſo much as ſee a play.
Nay which is more, he hath not ſeene great Hunckes,
Nor yet hath bin in Shor-ditch mongſt his Punckes.
And God forgiue him he is not preciſe,
Much to frequent any good exerciſe.
Why this is ſtrange a riddle not a rime,
Where hath this gallant yonker ſpent his time.
To tell the Ieſt I thinke t'will make you ſmile,
He hath bin inthe Counter all this while.

One

## *Epigram.*

ONe tolde a Courſer where he ſhould repayre,
And finde a field wel fraught with praunſing ware
Whither he went without let or denyall
Before he bought, thinking to ſteale a tryall.
Some two or three he backes, but doth reiourne,
The dull pac'd Iades they wold not ſerue his turne.
At laſt he back'd one, whoſe heeles did rebound,
As if his vaultage ſeemde to ſcorne the ground.
And though his rider keept him on the racke,
Ran quight away, his chapman on his backe:
His courage was of ſuch a fierie pitch,
As bore the Courſer ouer hedge and ditch.
But ſeeing one he feared would reueale him,
He raygn'd him in, he did not meane to ſteale him
It was the owner, then he keepes a ſturre,
Houlds backe his head, but giues his ſides the Spurre.
As if indeede he could not holde him ſtill,
But that he ſtole a Horſe againſt his will.
Nothing but this, yet he was hang'd they ſay,
Becauſe the horſe did carrie him away.

B

Doe

## *Epigram.*

Doe you knowe this fellowe in the veluet Iacke?
His first beginning was with, what doe ye lacke?
But now indeede the man in age doth droppe,
Therefore vnfit to keepe a Trades-mans Shoppe.
And he hath found the trade of bonds and libles,
The Deuill found it for his owne Desciples.
A Vsurer, O Sir tis verie true!
A faithfull villaine and an honest Iewe.
He will not sticke to lend his money foorth,
So hee haue pawne for fiue times more then worth.
Hee'le lend you money vppon all your state,
Be it in Landes, in Iewels, or in plate.
Heele smooth you vp, and speake you wondrous faire,
Pay when you can some weekes shall breake no square.
Trust not his kindenesse, then your case is euill,
As good to be behoulding to the Deuill.

If

## Epigram.

IF you to knowe this gallant doe defire,
Hee is the offpring of a couetous fire,
No fooner is the Father dead, fcarce colde,
But his braue Sonne beguilds his purfe with golde.
Vnto his Fathers Cloffet doth he hie,
In faith he longs to fee thefe Angelles flie.
Where like fome potent fellowe in his fumes,
Ruffles his feathers and difplayes his plumes.
And for his fignet takes his fathers ring
Angel his fubjeĉts; O moft gallant King.
To whome as one to pittie onely bent,
(Saithhe) I long beway'd your prifonment.
My father he kept you in flauerie,
But I am come to giue you libertie,
Next he takes care if he fhall liue or not,
To fpend the wealth his couetous Father got.

B 2                              Good

Good faith tis trewe his worſhippe lackes a man,
Heele make a ſhift heele ſpend it if he can.
Ten pound a yeare heele giue,each day three meales,
Onely to carrie golde after his heeles.
To beare foorth preſents,bee his apple ſquire,
To make a legge, and ſay *Ouy Mounſire*.
This being done out of the doores hee throwes,
To ſeeke companions my young Maſter goes.
Some twentie pound this day he doth disburſe,
He ſcornes to bring home fragments in his purſe,
Ere long his father muſt be layde in clay,
And then he ſweares heele make that day a day,
All the good Lads in England at the leaſt,
Muſt lend their preſence for to grace his feaſt,
Thus euerie day he reuels and makes ſporte,
Why he doth well his Kingdome is but ſhort.

But

## *Epigram.*

BVt who is this that commeth creeping heere,
That like the King of Hunger doth appeare.
O tis the braue resolued Gentleman,
That taketh Phisicke therefore looketh wan,
A strong purgation, hee hath had of late,
It purg'd his Purse and hath refind his state.
His purpose is to liue at rest and quiet,
Therefore hath bound himselfe to keepe a diet.
For these a weeke he doth abstaine to eate,
Not for deuotion, but for lacke of meate,
Alas good prodigall he knowes not where to dine,
His ordinarie is amongst the swine.
I was a foole (quoth hee) to thinke this thing,
That golden Angells had bin lame of wing.

Whose

*VVho dares not trust his wife before his eye:*
*A borne plague meetes him for his Iealousie.*

## Epigram.

A Fellowe once diseased in the head,
Liu'd much in doubt that he was cuckoled,
He asked counsell of his neighbor by,
If any meanes there were the truth to trie᾽
His friend comes ore him with a wondrous storie,
Of Saint *Lukes* share the Cuckoldes consistorie.
And sayes i'ft please him thither to repayre,
All night to inuocate that Saint with prayer,
If it were so, he did assure him well,
Ere morning come the Oracle would tell.
Till night was come my foole liu'd in confusion,
He was afuer to trie this strange conclusion,
Well hee is shipped off at Lyon kaye,
For his boone voyage at Saint *Lucas* baye.
He landed, doth vnto the alter goe
Whereon amaz'd he saw great hornes to growe.
He makes his prayer, tels the poste his plight,
All a colde, long, and teadiouse winter night.

                                          And

And euerie night-Bird that he hear'd to creake,
He still suppos'd the Oracle would speake.
Meane while his friend(he did before importune)
Supplide his roome and gaue my foole his fortune.
Well, morne is come no voice that hee can heare,
Hee thankes the Saint that his good wife is cleere.
Hauing performed his obsequious rightes,
Forthwith is dub'd one of Saint *Lucas* Knights.
Tis for his praise I hope, hee hath ingroste,
A payre of hornes more on Saint *Lucas* poste.
Increast himselfe although his wit was worne,
For he returned heauier by the horne.
Well home he comes thinking to take a nappe,
Alas his head had quight out growen his cappe.
This made him wonder but his wife was cleene,
He rather thought *Diana* he had seene.

A Poore

*Epigram.*

A Poore Slaue once with penurie afflicted,
Yet to Tobacco mightily adicted·
Sayes, they that take Tobacco keepes their health,
Are worthie fellowes in a common wealth.
For if (sayth he) Tobacco were our cheare,
Then other victuals neuer would be deere.
Fye on excesse it makes men faint and meeke,
A pennie loafe might serue a man a weeke.
Were we conform'd to the Camelions fare,
To liue by smoake as they doe liue by ayre.
O how our men oppresse and spoyle their sence,
in making hauoke of the elements.
He can giue reason for what he hath spoake,
My Salamander liues by fire and smoake.
Necessitie doth cause him to repeate,
Tobaccos praise for want of other meate.

A Iolly

## *Epigram.*

A Iolly fellow Eſſex borne and bred,
A Farmers Sonne his Father being dead,
T'expell his griefe and melancholly paſſions,
Had vowd himſelfe to Trauell and ſee faſhions.
His great mindes obieƈ was no trifling toy,
But to put downe the wandring Prince of Troy,
Londons diſcouerie, firſt he doth decide,
His man muſt be his Pilot and his guide.
Three miles he had not paſt, there he muſt ſit:
He ask't if he were not neere London yet?
His man replies, good Sir your ſelfe beſturre,
For we haue yet to goe ſixe times as farre.
Alas I had rather ſtay at home and digge,
I had not thought the worlde was halfe ſo bigge.
Thus this great worthie comes backe thoe with ſtrife,
he neuer was ſo farre in all his life.
None of the ſeauen worthies : on his behalfe,
Say, was not he a worthie Eſſex Calfe?

C          A Gentleman

## The Humors that haunt a VVife.

A Gentleman a verie friend of mine,
Hath a young wife and she is monstrous fine,
Shee's of the newe fantastique humor right,
In her attire an angell of the light.
Is she an Angell? If it may be well,
Not of the light, she is a light Angell.
Forsooth his doore must suffer alteration,
To entertaine her mightie huge Bom-fashion,
A hoode's to base, a hat which she doth male,
With brauest feathers in the Estridge tayle.
She scornes to treade our former proud wiues races,
That put their glorie in their owne faire face,
In her conceite it is not fayre enough
She must reforme it with your painters stuffe,
And she is neuer merrie at the heart,
Till she be got into her leatherne Cart.
Some halfe a mile the Coach-man guides the raynes,
Then home againe, birlady she takes paines.
My friend seeing what humors haunt a wife,
If he weare loose would leade a single life.

Next

## A Poore Mans pollicy.

NExt I will tell you of a poore mans tricke,
Which he did practise with a polliticke,
This poore man had a Cowe twas all his stocke,
Which on the Commons fed : where Catell flocke,
The other had a steere a wanton Beast,
Which he did turne to feede amongst the rest.
Which in processe although I knowe not how,
The rich mans Oxe did gore the poore mans Cow.
The poore man heereat vexed waxed sad,
For it is all the liuing that he had,
And he must loose his liuing for a song,
Alas he knew not how to right his wrong.
He knew his enemie had pointes of law,
To saue his purse, fill his deuouring mawe,
Yet thought the poore man how so it betide,
Ile make him giue right sentence on my side.

C 2                    Without

Without delay vnto the Man he goes,
And vnto him this feyned tale doth gloze,
(Quoth he)my Cowe which with your Oxe did feede,
Hath kild your Oxe and I make knowne the deede.
Why(quoth my Politique)thou fhouldft haue helpt it
Thou fhalt pay for him if thou wert my father. (rather,
The courfe of lawe in no wife muft be ftayde,
Leaft I an euill prefident be made.
O Sir (quoth he!) I cry you mercie nowe,
I did miftake,your Oxe hath gorde my Cowe.
Conuict by reafon he began to brawle,
But was content to let his action fall.
As why?(quoth he)thou lookft vnto her well,
Could I preuent the mifcheife that befell?
I haue more weightie caufes now to trie.
Might orecomes right without a reafon why.

                                            One

## Epigram.

ONe of the damned crew that liues by drinke,
  And by Tobacco's ftillified ftinke
Met with a Countrie man that dwelt at Hull
Thought he this peafant's fit to be my Gull.
His firft falute like to the French-mans wipe,
Wordes of encounter, pleafe you take a pipe.
The Countrieman amazed at this rable,
Knewe not his minde yet would be conformable.
Well in a petty Ale-houfe they enfconce
His Gull muft learne to drinke Tobacco once.
Indeede his purpofe was to make a ieft,
How with Tobacco he the peafant dreft.
Hee takes a whiffe, with arte into his head,
The other ftandeth ftill aftonifhed.
Till all his fences he doth backe reuoke,
Sees it afcend much like Saint Katherins fmoake.

C 3                    But

But this indeede made him the more admire,
He saw the smoke : thought he his head's a fyer,
And to increase his feare he thought poore soule,
His scarlet nose had been a fyerie cole.
Which circled round with Smoke, seemed to him
Like to some rotten brand that burneth dim.
But to shew wisdome in a desperat case,
He threw a Can of beere into his face,
And like a man some furie did inspire,
Ran out of doores for helpe to quench the fire.
The Ruffin throwes away his Trinidado,
Out comes huge oathes and then his short poynado,
But then the Beere soe troubled his eyes,
The countrie man was gon ere he could rise,
A fier to drie him he doth now require,
Rather then water for to quench his fire.

                           Come

## Epigram.

Come my braue gallant come vncafe, vncafe,
Neare fhall Obliuion your great actes deface.
He has been there where neuer man came yet,
An vnknowne countrie, I, ile warrant it,
Whence he could Ballace a good fhip inholde.
With Rubies, Saphers, Diamonds and golde,
Great Orient Pearles efteem'd no more then moates,
Sould by the pecke as chandlers meafure oates,
I meruaile then we haue no trade from thence,
O tis to far it will not beare expence.
Twere far indeede, a good way from our mayne,
If charges eate vp fuch exceffiue gaine,
Well he can fhew you fome of Lybian grauel,
O that there were another world to trauel,
I heard him fweare that hee (twas in his mirth)
Had been in all the corners of the earth.

                                        Let

Let all his wonders be together ſtitcht,
He threw the barre that great *Alcides* pitcht:
But he that ſawe the Oceans fartheſt ſtrands,
You poſe him if you aske where Douer ſtands.
He has been vnder ground and hell did ſee
*Aeneas* neare durſt goe ſo farre a hee.
For he hath gone through *Plutos* Regiment,
Saw how the Feindes doe Lyers there torment.
And how they did in helles damnation frye,
But who would thinke the Traueller would lye?
To dine with *Pluto* he was made to tartie,
As kindely vs'd as at his Ordinarie.
Hogſheades of wine drawne out into a Tub,
Where hee did drinke hand-ſmooth with *Belzebub*,
And *Proſerpine* gaue him a goulden bow
Tis in his cheſt he cannot ſhew it now.

One tould

## Of one that cousned the Cut-purse.

ONe toulde a Drouer that beleeu'd it not,
What booties at the playes the Cut-purse got,
But if' twere so my Drouers wit was quicke,
He vow'd to serue the Cut-purse a new tricke.
Next day vnto the play, pollicy hy'd,
A bagge of fortie shillings by his side,
Which houlding fast hee taketh vp his stand,
If stringes be cut his purse is in his hand.
A fine conceited Cut-purse spying this,
Lookt for no more, the fortie shillings his,
Whilst my fine Politique gazed about,
The Cut-purse feately tooke the bottom out.
And cuts the strings, good foole goe make a iest,
This Dismall day thy purse was fairely blest.
Houlde fast good Noddy tis good to dreade the worse,
Your monie's gone, I pray you keepe your purse.
The Play is done and foorth the foole doth goe,
Being glad that he cousned the Cut-purse soe.
He thought to iybe how he the Cut-purse drest,
And memorize it for a famous iest.
But putting in his hand it ran quight throw
Dash't the conceite, heele neuer speake on't now,
You that to playes haue such delight to goe,
The Cut-purse cares not, still deceiue him so.

D                    Dicke

## A drunken fray.

Dicke met with Tom in faith it was their lot,
Two honeſt Drunkards muſt goe drinke a pot.
Twas but a pot or ſay a little more,
Or ſay a pot that,s filled eight times ore.
But beeing drunke, and met well with the leeſe,
They drinke to healthes deuoutly on their knees,
Dicke drinkes to Hall to pledge him Tom reiectes,
And ſcornes to doe it for ſome odde reſpects
Wilt thou not pledge him, that'ᵴ a gull, a Scab,
Wert with my man-hood thou deſerueſt a ſtab,
But tis no matter drinke another bout,
Weele intot'h field and there weele trie it out.
Lets goe (ſaies Tom) no longer by this hand,
Nay ſtay (quoth Dicke) lets ſee if we can ſtand.
Then ſoorth they goe after the Drunken pace,
Which God he knowes was with a reeling grace,
Tom made his bargaine, thus with bonnie Dicke
If it ſhould chance my foote or ſo ſhould ſlipp,
How wouldſt thou vſe me or after what Size,
Wouldſt pare me ſhorter or wouldſt let me riſe,
Nay God forbid our quarrells not ſo great,
To kill thee on aduantage in my heate.

                                        Tuſh

Tush weele not fight for any hate ot foe,
But for meere loue that each to other owe.
And for thy learning loe Ile shew a tricke,
No sooner spoke the worde but downe comes Dicke,
Well now (quoth Tom)thy life hangs on my sword,
If I were downe how wouldst thou keepe thy worde?
Why with these hilts I'de braine thee at a blow,
Faith in my humor cut thy throate or foe,
But Tom he scornes to kill his conquered foe,
Lets Dicke arise and too't againe they goe.
Dicke throwes downe Tom or rather Tom did fall,
My hilts (quoth Dicke) shall braine thee like a maull.
Is't so (quoth Tom good faith what remedie,
The Tower of Babelles fallen and soe am I
But Dicke proceedes to giue the fatall wound,
It mist his throate : but run into the ground.
but he supposing that the man was slaine,
Straight fled his countrie, shipt himselfe for Spaine,
Whilst valiant Thomas dyed dronken deepe,
Forgot his danger and fell fast a sleepe.

D 2                                    What

## *Epigram.*

WHats he that ſtares as if he were afright? (ſpright
    The fellowe Sure hath ſeene ſome dreadfull
Maſſe rightly gueſt, why ſure I did diuine,
Hee's haunted with a Spirit feminine.
In plaine termes thus, the Spirit that I meane,
His martiall wife that notable curſt queane,
No other weapons but her nailes or fiſt,
Poore patient Ideot he dares not reſiſt,
His neighbor once would borrow buthis knife,
Good neighbor ſtay (quoth hee) ile aske my wife.
Once came he home Inſpired in the head,
Hee found his neighbor and his wife a bed,
Yet durſt not ſturre, but hide him in a hole,
He feared to diſpleaſe his wife poore ſole.
But why ſhould he ſo dreade and feare her hate,
Since ſhe had giuen him armour for his pate?
Next day forſooth he doth his neighbor meete,
Whome with ſterne rage thus furiouſly doth greete,
Villaine ile ſlit thy noſe, out comes his knife,
Sirra (quoth he) goe to Ile tell your wife.
Apaled at which terror meekely ſaide
Retire good knife my furie is all laide.

                                        Time

## Proteus.

TIme feruing humour thou wrie-faced Ape,
That canft transforme thy felfe to any fhape;
Come good *Proteus* come away apace,
We long to fee thy mumping Antique face.
This is the fellow that liues by his wit,
A cogging knaue and fawning Parrafit,
He has behauiour for the greateft porte,
And hee has humors for the rafcall forte,
He has been greate with Lordes and high eftates,
They could not liue without his rare conceites,
He was affociat for the braueft fpirits,
His gallant carriage fuch fauour merrits.
Yet to a Ruffin humor for the ftewes,
A right graund Captaine of the damned crewes,
With whome his humour alwaies is vnftable
Mad, melancholly, drunke and variable.

D 3

Hat

Hat without band like cutting Dicke he go'es,
Renowned for his new iuuented oathes.
Sometimes like a Ciuilian tis ſtrange
At twelue a clocke he muſt vnto the Change,
Where being thought a Marchant to the eye,
Hee tels ſtrange newes his humor is to lie.
Some Damaske coate the effect thereof muſt heare,
Inuites him home and there he gets good cheare.
but how is't now such braue renowned wits,
Weare ragged robes with ſuch huge gaſtly ſlitts,
Faith thus a ragged humor he hath got
Whole garments for the Summer are to hot.
Thus you may cenſure gently if you pleaſe,
He weares ſuch Garments onely for his eaſe.
Or thus, his creadit will no longer waue.
For all men know him for a prating knaue.

Vaniſh

## *Epilogue.*

VAnish ye hence ye changelings of the night,
For I descry your enemie the light:
Flye through the westerne Gate see you darke gleames,
Least in the east you meete with Phœbus beames
Descend into your Orbes I say begon,
And thanke your gentle Master Oberon.
Tell him how well your gestures fit our rime,
being roughly model d in so skert a time.
For what you see presented to your sight,
I onely write to tyer out the night,
Wherein if you delight to heere me sing
Weele haue more trafique with the fayrie King. E. M.

### FINIS.

# THE BRIDE

## BY S. R.

LONDON
Printed By W. I. for T. P. 1617.

# THE BRIDE TO
## ALL MAYDES.

*Not out of bubble blasted Pride,*
*Doe I oppose my selfe a Bride,*
*In scornefull manner with vpbraides:*
*Against all modest virgin maides.*
*As though I did dispise chast youth,*
*This is not my intent of truth,*
*I know they must liue single liues,*
*Before th'are graced to be wiues.*
*But such are only touch'd by me,*
*That thinke themselues as good as wee:*
*And say girles, weomens fellows arr,*
*Nay sawcely, Our betters farr:*
*Yea will dispute, they are as good,*
*Such wenches vex me to the blood,*
*And are not to be borne with all:*
*Those I doe here in question call,*
*whome with the rules of reasons Arte:*
*Ile teach more wit before we part.*
*Sylence, of kindnes I beseech,*
*Doe you finde eares, and weele finde speach.*

# THE BRIDE.

VIrgins, and fellow maydes ( that were of late)
Take kindly heere my weeding dayes a dew,
I entertayne degree aboue your ſtate:
For Marriage life's beyond the ſingle crew,
   Bring me to Church as cuſtome ſayes you ſhall,
   And then as wife, farewell my wenches all.

I goe before you vnto Honour now,
And *Hymen's* Rites with ioy doe vndertake
For life, I make the conſtant Nuptiall vow,
Striue you to follow for your credits ſake,
   For greater grace to Womankind is none
   Then Ioyne with husband, faithfull two in one.

God Honoured thus, our great Grand-mother *Eue*
And gaue thereby the bleſſing of increaſe,
For were not mariage we muſt all beleeue,
The generations of the earth would ceaſe.
   Mankind ſhould be extinguiſh'd and decreaſ'd
   And all the world would but conſiſt of beaſt.

Which cauſed me to finde my Mayden folly,
And having found it, to reforme the ſame:
     A 3         Though

# *The Bride.*

Though some of you, thereat seeme melanch ol y
That I for ever doe renounce your name.
  I not respect what censure you can giue,
  Since with a loving Man I meane to liue.

Whose kindest heart, to me is worth you all,
Him to content, my soule in all things seekes,
Say what you please, exclaiming chide and brall,
Ile turne disgrace vnto your blushing cheekes.
  I am your better now by *Ring* and *Hatt*,
  No more playn *Rose*, but *Mistris* you know what.

Marrie therefore and yeald increase a store,
Else to what purpose weare you breed and borne.
Those that receaue, and nothing giue therefore:
Are fruitles creatures, of contempt and scorne,
  The excellence of all things doth consist,
  In giuing, this no reason can resist.

The glorious Sun , in giving forth his light,
The Earth in plants, and hearbs & countles things
The trees their fruit, The *Empresse* of the Night
*She* bountious giues to rivers flouds and springs,
  And all that heaven, and all that earth containes,
  Their goodnes, in Increase of guifts explaynes.

But what doe you that neither giue nor take,
(As only made for hearing, and for seeing,)
Although created helpers for Mans sake:
                      Yet

# The Bride.

Yet Man no whit the better for your being,
  That spend consume and Idle out your howers,
  Like many garden-paynted vseleſſe flowers.

Your liues are like thoſe worthles barren trees,
That neuer yeald ( from yeare to yeare)but leaues:
Greene-bowes vpon them only all men ſees,
But other goodnes there is none receaues,
  They flouriſh ſommer and they make a ſhowe,
  Yet to themſelues they fruitles ſpring & growe.

Conſider beaſt, and fiſh and foule, all creatures,
How there is male and female of their kinde,
And how in loue they doe inlarge their natures:
Even by conſtrayn'd neceſſity inclyn'd:
  To paire and match, and couple tis decreed,
  To ſtocke and ſtore the earth, with what they
                                        (breed.
In that moſt powerfull word, ſtill power doth lye,
To whoſe obedience all muſt ſubiect bee,
That ſayd at firſt, *Increaſe and multiply*,
Which ſtill enduers from age to age we ſee:
  Dutie obligeth every one ſhould frame,
  To his dread will, that did commaund the ſame.

*It is not good for Man to be alone*,           beſt )
( Sayd that great God, who only knowes whats
And therefore made a wife of *Adams* bone,
While he repoſing ſlept, with quyet reſt,
                                        Which

# *The Bride.*

Which might prefage, the great Creator men.
In their coniunction, fume of earths content,

## *Miftris Sufan.*

Good *Miftris Bride,* now we haue hard your fpeach
In commendation of your Nuptiall choyfe,
Giue me a little favour I befeech,
To fpeake vnto you with a Virgins voyce:
   Though diuers elder maydes in place there be,
   Yet ile begin, trufting they'le fecond me.

We are your fellows but to Church you fay,
As cuftome is that maydes, fhould bring the *Bride,*
And for no longer then the wedding day,
You bould with vs, but turne to tother fide:
   Boafting of Honour you affend vnto,
   And fo goe forward making much adoe.

But this vnto you Iuftly I obiect,
In the defence of each beloued mayde,
*Virginity,* is life of chaft refpect,
No worldly burden thereupon is layd:
   Our fyngle life, all peace and quiet bringes,
   And we are free from carefull earthly things.

We may doe what we pleafe, goe where we lift,
Without pray *husband will you giue me leaue,*
Our refolutions no man can refift,

                Our

# *The Bride.*

Onr own's our owne, to giue or to receiue,
  We liue not vnder this same word obay:
  *Till Death depart vs,*at our dying day.

We may delight in fashion,weare the same,
And chuse the stuffe of last devised sale:
Take Taylors counsell in it free from blame,
And cast it off assoone as it growes stale:
  Goe out, come in,and at selfe pleasure liue,
  And kindly take, what kind youngmen do giue.

Wee haue no checking churlish taunts to feare vs,
We haue no grumbling at our purse expence:
We seeke no misers favour to forbeare vs,
We vse no houshold wranglings and offence:
  We haue no cocke to over crowe our combe,

### *Cate.*

Well said good *Susan,*now thou pay'st her home.

### *Bride.*

A little favour pray,good *Mistris Sue,*
You haue a time to heare aswell as speake:
You challenge more by odds then is your due,
And stand on Arguments are childish weake:
  Of freedome,liberty,and all content,
  But in the aire your breath is vainely spent.

B                 It

# *The Bride.*

It is your shame to bost you haue your will,
And that you are in feare of no controwle,
Your cases *Susan*, are more bad and ill,
Most dangerous to body and to soule:
  A woman to her will hath oft bin try'd,
  To run with errour, on the left hand side.

Pray did not danger then to *Eue* befall,
When she tooke liberty without her heda,
The *Serpent* ouercame her therwithall,
And thorow will, she wilfull was misled:
  Yelding assoone as *Sathan* did intice,
  And of her husband neuer tooke aduise.

In wit to men we are inferiour far,
For arts for learning, and Ingenious things,
No rare Inuentions in our braynes there are,
That publique profit to a kingdome brings:
  Tis they that must all callings execute,
  And wee of all their labours reape the fruite.

They are Diuines for soules true happines,
They Maiestraites to right offensiue wronges,
They souldiers for their martiall valiantnes,
They artizans, for all to vse belonges:
  They husbandmen to worke the earths increase,
  And they the some of womens ioye and peace.

And shall not we performe obedience then.

                   As

# *The Bride.*

As wee are bound by law of God and nature,
Yealding true harts affection vnto men,
Ordain'd to rule and gouerne euery creature:
  Why then of all on earth that liue and moue,
  We fhould degenerate and monfters proue.

*Beſſe.*

Monfters (forfoth) nere fleepe in maidens beds,
But they are lodged with your married wiues,
The knotty browes,and rugged butting heds,
Concerne not vs,profeffing fingle liues,
  To learne your horne-booke we haue no deuotiō
  Keepe monfters to your felues,we fcorne the mo-
                                     (tion.

*Bride.*

Beffe,of fuch fhapes, whē your turne coms to mar-
A carefull mynd,in choyfe of husband beare, (ty
For if your browes from former fmothnes varry,
Thinke on this fpeach, *It commeth with a feare :*
  Which I am paft,perplexe me no feare can.
  Being fure I haue a conftant honeft man.

*Iane.*

Belieue you haue,and t'is enough they fay,
But you and I agree not in a mynde,
I read in ftoryes men will run aftray,
           B 2                   Yet

# *The Bride.*

Yet make their foolish wiues beleeue th'are kind:
  And therefore since they are so cunning knowne
  Ile keepe my selfe a maide and trust to none.

Had I one sutor swore himselfe loue-sicke,
Another for his Mistris sake would die,
A third thorow *Cupids* power growne lunaticke,
A fourth that languishing past hope did lye :
  And so fift, sixt, and seauenth in loues passion,
  My Maiden-head for them should ner'e change
                          (fashion.

*Æneas* told many a cogging tale,
To *Dido* that renowned worthy Queene,
And *Iason* with his flatterings did preuaile,
Yet falser knaues in loue were neuer seene:
  And at this instant hower, as they were then,
  The world aboundeth with deceitfull men.

*Doll.*

*Iane,* thats too true, for to you all I sweare,
How I was bobd by one tis shame to tell,
A smoother fellow neuer wench did heare,
And as I liue, I thought he lou'd me well :
  Heere you shall see one of his cunning letters,
  Which still I keepe, & meane to shew his betters.

In Romane hand, on guilded paper writ,

                             Pray

## The Bride.

Pray *Dorothy* read you it to the reſt,
But whether his owne head inuented it,
Or robd ſome printed Booke, I doe proteſt :
  I cannot tell, but his owne name is to it,
  Which proues he takes vpon him for to doe it.

---

## The Loue Letter.

*The trueſt heart, ſhall nought but falſhood cheriſh,*
*The mildeſt man, a cruell tyrant prooue,*
*The water drops, the hardeſt flint ſhall periſh,*
*The hilles ſhall walke, and maſsie earth remooue:*
  *The brighteſt Sun ſhall turne to darkeſome clowde,*
  *Ere I prooue falſe, where I my loue haue vowde.*

*Ere I prooue falſe, the world deſolu'd ſhall be,*
*To that ſame nothing that it was before,*
*Ere I prooue falſe mine eyes ſhall ceaſe to ſee,*
*And breath of life ſhall breath in me no more :*
  *The ſtrong built frame ſhall moue from his foundati-*
  *Ere I remoue my ſoules determination.*     *(on*

*Death ſhall forget to kill, and men to dye,*
*Condemned ſoules ſhall laugh, and ceaſe to mourne,*
*The loweſt hell ſhall riſe and meete the ſkye,*
*Time ſhall forget his courſe and backe returne :*
  *Contrary vnto kinde each thing ſhall proue,*

                                   *Ere*

# The Bride.

*Ere I be falfe or once forget my loue.*

*Oh then deare heart regard my fad eftate,*
*My pafsions griefe and wofull lamentation,*
*Oh pittie me ere pittie come too late,*
*That hold thee deare paft mans imagination:*
    *Preferue my life and fay that thou wilt haue me,*
    *Or elfe I die the whole world cannot faue me.*

### Grace.

This is a Ballad I haue heard it fung.

### Doll.

Well, be or be not, that's not to the matter,
But who will truft a louers pen or tongue,
That vfe all proteftations thus to flatter:
    For this bafe fellow that was fo perplext,
    Sent this one monday, and was married next.

### Sara.

Now out vpon him moft diffembling creature,
Ile warrant you that he can neuer thriue,
He fhowes himfelfe, euen of as bad a nature,
As euer was in any man aliue:
    Alas poore foole that hath this fellow got,
    Shee hath a Iewell of him, hath fhe not?

*Noll*

# *The Bride.*

### *Nell.*

Yes furely hath fhe,(waying all things deepe,)
A louer that will taft as fweete as gall,
One that is better farre to hang then keepe,
And I perfwade me you doe thinke fo all:
   Excepting onely partiall *Miftris Bride,*
   For fhe ftands ftoutly to the married fide.

### *Bride.*

So farre as reafon,and as right requires,
I will defend them both by word and deede,
Yet haue I no apology for lyers,
And ill conditions that falfe hearts doe breede :
   " All that are married be not faithfull kinde,
   " Nor all vnmarried,are not chaft in minde.

Are there not maids(vpon your côfcience fpeake?)
Knowne to your felues as well as you knowe me,
Will vowe their loue to men,and falfly breake,
Which in the number of your *Virgins* be,
   That will delude fome halfe a fcore young men,
   And hauing gull'd them,take fome other then.

I will not name her was in loue with ten,
But in your eares i'le note her fecret ; harke,
She had both Courtiers,Cockneys,Country-men,
Yet in the ende a Saylor boards her Barke :
   And therefore put not men in all the blame,
   But fpeake the trueth,and fo the diuell fhame.
                      *Grace.*

# *The Bride.*

### *Grace.*

I knowe the partie well that you doe meane,
And thus much for her I dare boldly fay,
To diuers futors though fhe feemed to leane,
To trye her fortunes out the wifeft way:
   Yet did fhe neuer plight her faith to any,
   But vnto him fhe had, among fo many :

And ther's no doubt but diuers doe as fhe,
Your felfe in confcience, haue had more then one,
To whom in fhewe you would familiar be,
And comming to the point why you would none:
Ciuilitie allowes a courteous cariage,
To fuch as proffer loue by way of marriage.

An affable behauiour may be vfed,
And kinde requitall anfwere kinde defeart,
And yet no honeft man thereby abufed,
With fained fhowes, as if he had the heart :
   When there is purpofe of no fuch intent
   To gull him with his time and mony fpent.

### *Mall.*

Were I to giue maides counfell, they to take it,
And that they would confent to doe as I,
Who offered vs his loue, we would forfake it,
And like *Dianes Nymphs* would liue and die:
                           For

# *The Bride.*

For I proteſt your louers ſhould haue none,
But wiues and widdowes to put tricks vpon.

We would reuenge the crafty double dealing,
Thouſands of harmeleſſe virgins doe endure,
By their deceitfull art of kinde-hart ſtealing,
Keeping our loues vnto our ſelues ſecure :
   And credit to their vowes,ſhould be no other,
   But in at one eare, and goe out at t'other.

*Bride.*

This you would doe, and y'are in that minde now,
But I perſwade me tis but raſhly ſpoken,
And therefore *Mary* make no fooliſh vow,
For if you doe in conſcience t'will be broken :
   Say you doe meane to keepe you free from man,
   But to be ſure,ſtill put in *If you can.*

Or elſe you may preſume aboue your power,
Twixt words and deedes,   great difference often
You may be taken ſuch a louing hower, (growes,
Your heart may all be *Cupids* to diſpoſe :
   Then vve ſhall haue you ſicke,& pine and grieue,
   And nothing but a husband can relieue.

Aske but your elders that are gone before,
And the'le ſay marry maide as we haue done,
Twixt twelue and twenty open loue the doore,
And ſay you vvere not borne to liue a Nonne:
         C           vnperfect

# *The Bride.*

Vnperfect female, liuing odde you are,
Neuer true euen, till you match and paire.

Iuſt-*Nature* at the firſt this courſe did take,
Woman and man deuided were in twaine,
But by vniting both did ſweetely make,
Deuiſions bliſſe contenfull to remaine,
   Which well made lawe of *Nature* and of kinde,
   To matters reaſonles doe nothing binde.

Nothing vnfit, nothing vniuſt to doe,
But all in order orderly conſiſting,
Then what ſeeme they that wil not ioine their two
And ſo be one, without vnkinde reſiſting:
   Surely no other cenſure paſſe I can,
   But ſhe's halfe woman liues without a man.

One, that depriues her ſelfe of whats her right,
Borne vnto care, and ignorant of eaſe,
A luſtleſſe liuing thing, without delight,
One, whom vnpleaſantneſſe beſt ſeemes to pleaſe:
   Depriu'd of lifes ſweete ioy, from kind remoued,
   Of worthleſſe parts, vnworthy to be loued.

Who will in paine pertake with ſuch a one,
(Whom we may moſt vnhappy creature call,)
Who will aſſiſt her, when her griefe makes mone,
Or who vphold her if ſhe chance to fall:
                    **The**

## The Bride.

The burthen one doth beare is light to two,
For twisted cordes are hardest to vndoe.

The loue and ioy doth absolute remaine,
That in posteritie is fixed fast,
For thou in children art new borne againe,
When yeeres haue brought thee to thy breath-
(spent last:
   Those oliue plants, shall from each other spring,
   Till *Times* full period endeth euery thing.

This being thus, what sencelesse girles you be,
To iustifie a life not worth embracing,
Opposing silly maiden wits gainst me,
That will not yeelde an ynch to your out-facing:
   For were heere present all the maydes in towne,
   With marriage reasons I would put them down.

### *Prudence.*

Kinke sisters all, now I haue heard the *Bride*,
Will you haue my opinion, not to flatter,
Sure I am turning to the wedding side,
I heare such good sound reason for the matter:
   Let *Grace, Doll, Besse* and *Susan, Mary, Iane,*
   Leade apes in hell, I am not of their vaine.

As sure as death ile ioyne my selfe with man,
C 2                 For

# *The Bride.*

For I perſwade me tis a happy life,
Ile be a Bride vvith all the ſpeede I can,
It's vvonder how I long to be a vvife:
*Grace* heer's good counſell,had you grace to take it
  *Suſan* tis ſound,oh *Beſſe* doe not forſake it.

Good husband-men vve ſee doe euer vſe,
To chuſe for forfit thoſe that breede the beſt,
And none vvill keepe bad breeders that can chuſe,
Euen ſo your fowlers that often brood the neſt,
  Are moſt eſteem'd,&their kinds worthieſt thoght
  All barren things,by all are counted nought.

Who plantes an orchard vvith vnfruitfull trees,
None but a madman ſo vvill vvaſt his ground,
Or vvho ſowes corne vvhere onely ſand he ſees,
Aſſured that there vvill no increaſe be found :
  And in a vvord all that the vvorld containes,
  Haue excellence in their begetting gaines.

For my part therefore I reſolue me thus,
Vnto the purpoſe I vvas borne,ile liue,
All maydes are fooles that vvill not ioyne vvith vs,
And vnto men their right of marriage giue :
  Moſt vvorthy Bride,here is my hand and vow,
  I loue a man in heart,as vvell as thou.
                    *Francis.*
*Prudence,*I am of your opinion iuſt,
A vvif's farre better then a matchleſſe maide,

                                        Ile

# *The Bride.*

Ile ftay no longer virgin then needes muft,
The law of Nature ought to be obayde:
    Either vve muft haue inward loue to men,
    Or elfe beare hate,and fo be brutifh then.

Doth not the vvorld inftruct vs this by others,
That vvedlocke is a remedy for finne,
Shall vve be vvifer then our reuerent mothers,
That married,or we all had baftards bin:
    And ere our mothers loft their maiden Iemme,
    Did not our grandhams euen as much for them.

From whence haue you the gift to liue vnwed,
Pray of what ftuffe are your ftraight bodies made,
By what chaft fpirit was your niceneffe bred,
That feeme of flefh to be fo purely ftayde:
    Are not all here made females for like ends,
    Fye,fye for fhame,difemble not with friends.

Ile tell you one thing which by proofe I knowe,
My mother had a cocke that vs'd to roame,
And all the hens would to our neighbours goe,
We could not keepe them for our liues at home:
    Abroad they went,though we woldnere fo faine
    Vntill by chance we got our cocke againe.

And fo my fathers pigeons in like fort,
Our matchleffe hens about would euer flye,
To paire with other doues they would refort,
(Pray laugh not *Sufan,*for it is no lye)

# The Bride.

I haue it not from other folkes·relation,
But from mine owne,and mothers obferuation.

### Sufan.

I laugh that you compare vs to your hens,
Or ftraying pigions that abroad haue flowne,
To feeke about for cocks of other mens,
Becaufe (you fay)they wanted of their owne :
 But *Francke*, though you like them be francke
         and free,
 You muft not iudge all other fo to be.

We doe not vfe to hunt abroad for cockes,
But rather fhun the places where they be,
The prouerbe fayes,*let geefe beware the fox*,
Tis eafie making prayes of fuch as we :
 That will not keepe them from the charmers
        (charme.
 Mens flatteries doe maiden-heads much harme.

### Bride.

Flatterers are of all to be reiected,
As well of wiues as you that are but maydes,
We praife not faults wherewith men are infected,
Nor yeeld applaufe to euery one perfwades :
 Our prayfing men thus vnderftand you muft,
 Tis meant of thofe are honeft, louing,iuft.
         Why

# *The Bride.*

Why there are men doe erre in what you hold,
Chaſt batchelers that neuer meane to match,
Who for the ſiugle life ſmooth tales haue told,
And yet the fleſhly knaues will haue a ſnatch:
    Ile ne're truſt thoſe that of them ſelues doe boaſt,
    The great'ſt preſiſians will deceiue you moſt.

I knew a prating fellow would maintaine,
A married man had but two merry dayes,
His wedding day the ioyfull firſt of twaine,
For then God giue you ioy, euen all men ſayes:
    The ſecond merry day of married life,
    Is that whereon he burieth his wife.

And woemen vnto ſhippes he would compare,
Saying as they continually lacke mending,
So wiues ſtill out of repairations are,
And vrge their husbands daily vnto ſpending:
    Yea worſe diſgrace, he would preſume to ſpeake:
    Which I will ſpare, leaſt I offend the weake.

But note the badneſſe of this wretches life,
That counted woemen abiect things forſaken,
He raune away at laſt with's neighbours wife,
Worthy of hanging were the raſcall taken:
    Such odious actes haue ſuch diſhoneſt mates,
    that againſt marriage, rude and ſenceles prates.

                              But

## *The Bride.*

But you moſt wilfull wenches that oppoſe,
Againſt the ſtate that you are borne to honour,
A propheſie vnto you Ile diſcloſe,
And ſhe that here doth take moſt nice vpon her:
   Pray note it well,for there is matter in it,
   And for to doe you good thus I beginne it.

When fiſh with fowle change elements together,
The one forſaking aire,the other water,
And they that woare the finne , to weare the fea-
                          (ther,
Remaining changelings all the worlds time after:
   The courſe of nature will be ſo beguilde,
   One maide ſhall get another maide with childe.

When euery Crow ſhall turne to be a Parret,
And euery Starre out-ſhine the glorious Sunne,
And the new water works runne white and clarret,
That come to towne by way of *Iſlington*,
   Woemen and men ſhall quite renounce each o-
                         (ther.
  And maides ſhall bee with childe, like *Merlins*
                         (mother.
     *Grace.*

Like *Merlins* mother,how was that I pray,
For I haue heard he was a cunning man,
There lines not ſnch another at this day,
   Nor euer was, ſince *Brittans* firſt began :

                              Tell

# *The Bride.*

Tell vs the ſtory,and we well will minde it.
Becauſe they ſay , *In written bookes we finde it.*

*Bride.*

Marry this *Merlins* mother was welſh Lady,
That liued in *Carnaruan* beautious maide,
And loue of Lords and Knights ſhee did not way
(by,
But ſet all light, and euery one denay'd :
　All Gentlemen, (as all you knowe be there,)
　That came a wooing were no wit the neere.

At length it hapned that this gallant girle,
Which ſcorned all men that ſhe euer ſaw,
Holding her ſelfe to be a matchleſſe Pearle,
And ſuch a Loadeſtone that could Louers draw :
　Grew belly-full,exceeding bigge and plumpe,
　Which put her Mayden-credit in a dumpe.

Time running courſe,and her full ſtomacke ſed,
When conſumation of fewe months expired,
Shee husbandleſſe,a mayde was brought to bed,

D
Of

# *The Bride.*

Of that rare *Merlin* that the world admired:
This to be honeſt,all her friends did doubt it,
Much prittle prattle was in *wales* about it.


So that ere long,the ſtrangnes of the thing,
To heare that Lady *Adhan* had a childe,
Caus'd famous *Arthur*,(being Brittans King)
Send for her to the Court,and reaſon milde :
   To know how this rare matter could be done,
   And make her finde a father for her ſonne.


She told his Maieſtie with ſighes and teares,
That keeping beautie carefull from the Sunne,
Within her chamber ſafely ſhut from feares,
Till *Phæbus* horſes to the Weſt wererunne :
   The doores faſt lock'd,and ſhe her ſelfe alone,
   Came in a gallant ſtranger, meere vnknowne.


Who euer came in courting manner to her,
With all the louing courage could be thought :
So powerfull in perſwaſions force to woe her,
That to his will conſtrained ſhe was brought :
   Although her heart did firme deniall vow,
   Yet ſhe was forc'd to yeeld and knew not how.

So

## The Bride.

So oft he came (quoth she) priuate and ſtrange,
When I ſhut vp my ſelfe in moſt ſad humor,
That I began to finde an inward change,
Which brought me quickly to an outward tumor:
　An't pleaſe your highnes I was in ſuch caſe,
　That to the world I durſt not ſhow my face.


My foes reioyced, all my friends were ſad,
My ſelfe in ſorrow ſpent both day and night,
No ſatisfaction my wrong'd honour had,
Was neuer maide in ſuch perplexed plight:
　To be with child whether I will or no,
　And for my child, no humane father know.


Had I bin married (quoth ſhe) as I ought,
And with my loue, the loue of man requited,
I had not to this woefull ſtate bin brought,
In all contempt, diſgracefully deſpighted:
　And tearmed ſtrumpet by the rude vnciuill,
　Who ſay my ſonne is baſtard to the diuell.


Wherefore I wiſh Ladies of my degree,
And all the reſt inferiour ſorts of maydes,
To take a warning (for their good) by me,

　　　　　Yeelding

# *The Bride.*

Yeelding affection when kind men perfwades :
  And hate difdaine that vile accurfed fin,
  Leaft they be plagu'd for pride as I haue bin.


How fay you to this warning wenches now,
That Lady *Adhan* giues vnto you all,
Were you not better marriage to allow,
Then in a manner for a Midwife call:
  I thinke you were if I might iudge the caufe,
  How fay you *Sufan*, fpeake good *Doll* and *Grace.*


*Grace.*

This is a ftory that feemes very ftrange,
And for my part, it doth me full perfwade,
My Mayden-head with fome man to exchange,
I will not liue in danger of a mayde:
  The world the flefh, the diuell tempts vs ftill,
  Ile haue a husband, I proteft I will.


If I were fure none of you here would blabbe,
I would euen tell you of a dreame moft true,
And if I lye, count me the verieft drabbe,
That euer any of you faw or knewe:

When

## *The Bride.*

When a friend fpeakes in kindnes do not wrong
                                        (her:
For I can keepe it (for my life) no longer.


One night (I haue the day of moneth fet downe)
Becaufe I will make ferious matters fure,
Me thought I went a iourney out of towne,
And with a propper man I was made fure :
 As fure as death, me thought we were affured,
 And all things for the bufineffe were procured.


We did agree, and faith and troath did plight,
And he gaue me, and I gaue him a Ring,
To doe as *Miftris Bride* will doe at night,
And I proteft me thought he did the thing :
 The thing we ftand fo much vpon he tooke;
 And I vpon the matter bigge did looke.


Forfooth (in fadnes,) I was bigge with childe,
And had a belly, (marry God forbid,)
Then fell a weeping, but he laught and fmil'd,
And boldly faid, weele ftand to what we did :
 Fye, fye (quoth I) who euer ftands I fall,
 Farewell my credit, maydenhead and all.

D 3       Thus

# *The Bride.*

Thus as I cry'd and wept and wrong my hands,
And faid deare maydes and maydenhead adue,
Before my face me thought my mother ftands,
And queftion'd with me how this matter grew :
   With that I ftart awake as we are now,
   Yet feard my dreame had bin no dreame I vow.


I could not (for my life) tell how to take it,
For I was ftricken in a mightie maze,
Therefore if marriage come Ile not forfake it,
Tis danger to liue virgin diuers wayes,
   I would not in fuch feare againe be found,
   Without a husband, for a thoufand pound.

*Sufan.*

Is it euen fo *Grace*, are you come to this,
You that perfwaded me from loue of late,
When you knew who, fent me a Ring of his :
And would haue had me bin his turtle mate,
   You cunningly did make me to forfake him,
   Becaufe I thinke in confcience you will take him.

Ile truft your word another time againe,
That can diffemble fo againft your heart,
Wifhing that I fhould earneftly refraine,

                From

# *The Bride.*

From that which thou thy felfe embracer art:
This is braue doing, I commend you *Grace*,
But ile nere truſt you more in ſuch a caſe.

*Bride.*

I pray you here let this contention ende,
(We being all of ſelfe ſame woman kind,)
And each the other, with aduiſe befriend,
Becauſe I ſee ſome of you well enclin'd :
   To take good wayes, and ſo become good wiues,
   Ile teach you certaine rules to leade your liues.

You that intend the honourable life,
And vvould vvith ioy liue happy in the ſame,
Muſt note eight duties doe concerne a wife,
To vvhich vvith all endeuour ſhe muſt frame :
   And ſo in peace poſſeſſe her husbands loue,
   And all diſtaſt from both their hearts remooue.

The firſt is that ſhe haue domeſtique cares,
Of priuate buſineſſe for the houſe vvithin,
Leauing her husband vnto his affaires,
Of things abroad that out of doores haue bin :
   By him performed as his charge to doe,
   Not buſie-body like inclin'd thereto.

Nor

## *The Bride.*

Nor intermedling as a number will,
Of foolifh goffips, fuch as doe negleƈt,
The things which doe concerne them, and too ill,
Prefume in matters vnto no effeƈt:
    Beyond their element, when they fhould looke,
    To what is done in Kitchin by the Cooke.

Or vnto childrens vertuous education,
Or to their maides that they good hufwiues be,
And carefully containe a decent fafhion,
That nothing paffe the lymmits of degree:
    Knowing her husbands bufineffe from her own,
    And diligent doe that, let his alone.

The fecond dutie of the wife is this,
(Which fhee in minde ought very carefull beare)
To entertaine in houfe fuch friends of his,
As fhe doth know haue husbands welcome there:
    Not her acquaintance without his confent,
    For that way Iealoufie breeds difcontent.

An honeft woman will the fcandall fhun,
Of that report is made of wantonneffe,
And feare her credit will to ruine run,

                  When

# *The Bride.*

When euill speakers doe her shame expresse :
And therefore from this rule a practise drawes,
That the effect may ceafe, remoue the caufe.


Th'ird dutie is, that of no proude pretence,
She moue her husband to confume his meanes,
With vrging him to needleffe vaine expence,
Which toward the Counter, or to Ludgate leanes :
   For many ydle huswiues (London knowes)
   Haue by their pride bin husbands ouerthrowes.


A modeft vvoman vvill in compaffe keepe,
And decently vnto her calling goe,
Not diuing in the frugall purfe too deepe,
By making to the world a pecocke fhowe : (wiues,
   Though they feeme fooles, fo yeelde vnto their
   Some poore men doe it to haue quiet liues.


Fourth dutie is, to loue her owne houfe beft,
And be no gadding goffippe vp and downe,
To heare and carry tales amongft the reft,
That are the newes reporters of the towne :
   A modeft vvomans home is her delight,
   Of bufineffe there, to haue the ouerfight.

E                      At

# *The Bride.*

At publike playes fhe neuer will be knowne,
And to be tauerne gueft fhe euer hates,
Shee fcornes to be a ftreete-wife(Idle one,)
Or field vvife ranging vvith her vvalking mates:
   She knows how wife men cenfure of fuch dames,
   And how with blottes they blemifh their good
                                (names.

And therefore with the doue fheele rather choofe,
To make aboade where fhe hath dwelling place,
Or like the fnayle that fhelly houfe doeth vfe,
For fhelter ftill,fuch is good-hufwiues cafe:
   Refpecting refidence where fhe doth loue,
   As thofe good houfholders,the fnayle and doue.

Fift dutie of a wife vnto her head,
Is her obedience to reforme his will,
And neuer with a felfe-conceit be led,
That her aduife prooues good,his counfell ill:
   In Iudgement being fingular alone,
   As hauing all the wit,her husband none.

She muft not thinke her wifedome to be thus,
(For we alaffe are weakelings vnto men)
What fingular good thing remaines in vs,

                         Of

# The Bride.

Of wife ones in a thoufand, fhow me ten,
  Her ftocke of wit, that hath the moft (I fay,)
  Hath fcarfe enough for fpending euery day.


When as the husband bargaines hath to make,
In things that are depending on his trade,
Let not wifes boldnes, power vnto her take,
As though no match were good but what fhe made
  For fhe that thus hath oare in husbands boate,
  Let her take breech, and giue him petti-coate.


Sixt dutie is, to pacifie his yre,
although fhe finde that he empatient be,
For hafty words, like fuell adde to fire,
And more, and more infenceth wraths degree:
  When fhe perceiues his choller in a fit,
  Let her forbeare, and that's a figne of wit.


Many occafions vnto men doe fall,
Of aduerfe croffes, woemen not conceiue,
To find vs honny, they doe meete with gall,
Their toyle for vs, doe their owne ioyes bereaue:
  Great fhame it were, that we fhould ad their woe,
  That doe maintaine, and keepe, and loue vs fo.

If

# *The Bride.*

If that a hasty word sometime be spoke,
Let vs not censure therefore they are foes,
Say tis infirmitie that doth prouoke,       (knowes:
Their hearts are sorry for their tongues God
   Since we by proofe each day and hower finde,
   For one harsh word, they giue ten thousand kind.


The seuenth dutie that she must endeauour,
Is to obserue her husbands disposition,
And thereunto conforme her selfe for euer,
In all obedient sort, with meeke submission:
   Resoluing that as his conditions are,
   Her rules of life she must according square.


His vertues and good parts which she doth finde,
shee must endeauor for to imitate,
The vices whereunto he is enclin'd,
Shee must in patience beare in milde estate:
   So that the meekenesse of her louing carriage,
   May be peace-maker, of all strife in marriage.


She must not doe as foolish woemen vse,
When they are met about the gossippes chat,
Their absent husbands with their tongues abuse,

                             But

## *The Bride.*

But vtterly abhorre to offer that :
   Refoluing that a husbands leaſt diſgrace,
   Sould cauſe the wife to haue a bluſhing face.


The eight laſt dutie ſhe muſt take vpon her,
To binde all t'other ſeauen to be done,
Is loue and chiefe regard to husbands honour,
Which if at true affection it begunne :
   Then be he poore, or ſicke, or in diſtreſſe,
   See ſtill remaines moſt firme in faithfulneſſe.


Beſt in aduerſitie it will appeare,
What conſtancy within the heart remaines,
No teſtimonie can be found more cleare,
Then friend in trouble rhat his loue explaines :
   For ſuch a one we may reſolue is true,
   That changeth not, though fortune turne from
                            (you.


And thus faire virgins, to you all farewell,
What I haue ſpoken doe proceede from loue,
The ioyes of marriage I want art to tell,
And therefore no more talke, but try and proue :
   With wedding rings, be wiues of credit knowne
   God ſend good husbands to you euery one.


*F I N I S.*